REBECAH

A Mother's Story

Jill Taylor

ATHENA PRESS
LONDON

REBECAH
A Mother's Story

ISBN 1 84401 256 5

First Published 2004 by
ATHENA PRESS
Queen's House, 2 Holly Road
Twickenham, TW1 4EG
United Kingdom

Printed for Athena Press

REBECAH

A Mother's Story

Dedicated to

Family:
Stuart, Rebecah, James, Carol, my sister,
and Mum for loving me.

Friends:
Dawn, Neil, Ellen, Mary, Kath, Joy, Maggie, Heather,
Kim, Jacquie, Sue, David, Rhona, Joyce, Renee, Jenny, Paul,
and Marielle who told me to write the book.

You chose deafness – do you know why?
Was it so that you could fly so high
Above the commonality of word
With thought unbroken – be really heard
In the strength of your own being
There for others – help their seeing?

Foreword

REBECAH IS DEAF AND HER STORY IS WRITTEN THROUGH MY eyes and ears, with the intention to touch the hearts of many. Events within her life are highlighted through poignant memories, underscored with a meaningful emotional charge and purpose in their telling. They are encapsulated under such headings as 'Funny Times' or 'Magic and Wonder' rather than being strictly chronologically told.

Delightfully, and in story form, my story emerges from as a natural progression of those deeper insights. This exotic adventure gives us an encapsulating yet penetrating synopsis of that inner purpose; that drive to know truth. The story culminates, ultimately, in connecting Rebecah's and my own life's purpose with a oneness of heart.

Finally, with both candour and humour, Rebecah's own account is written through her eyes and ears.

My Story

BEGINNING WITH 'EXOTIC ADVENTURES', I HAVE WOVEN together a number of different events that have occurred at different times throughout my life. Nearly all of these events are true (certainly the main ones are), and are absolutely true in their essence – which is why relaying them brought up such provocative emotions for me – but the characters are fictitious. However, as in most fiction, they are based on real people with one exception: the Shaman. He was purely from my imagination.

To give an example of what I mean, the walking on coals incident actually took place on the edge of my hometown in somebody's back garden about four years ago. The man presiding over the ceremony (represented as Carrie in the story), lit incense, washed our feet, read sacred words and walked on the coals several times himself. Rebecah joined me, and events occurred much as relayed in the chapter.

Rebecah's story is drawn from my memory banks and for obvious reasons is currently evolving. Two days ago my husband, Stuart, and I sat down to watch a video of 'News Week' presented in sign language by... Rebecah Taylor. Stuart always worried about Rebecah's future. I never did.

Introduction

THE CHALLENGES OF BRINGING UP A DEAF CHILD HAVE BEEN experienced by many, and in circumstances far tougher than my own. Add to that the children with some kind of impairment other than or in addition to deafness, or merely add to that the human challenge of just bringing up a child and we see the common bond we all share. As a race, parenthood is our saving grace. If we did for others what we do for our children, demonstrated the same degree of tolerance, forgiveness and unconditional love, the world would be different. When I remind myself of this I take a step back.

This step back, this re-evaluation has been a necessary journey. Without it things like humility, surrender, allowing and patience would have been that much harder to implement. And why do our children so readily teach us those things? The answer is simple: we love them.

This book is offered as a sharing of my life with you, the reader. I have dared to put in print some of my inner and outer struggles with Rebecah, and the joys too. I have dared to put into words some of my most profound experiences, so that you may perhaps realise that you've also experienced these things. When we share, something is opened up to both parties. When we overcome a deep struggle, there is that sense of profound joy and relief that we would not have experienced otherwise.

This, then, is my account of my life as the mother of Rebecah.

Magic and Wonder

Heaven lies about us in our infancy.

William Wordsworth

THERE ARE MANY STORIES CONVEYING THE DIVINE CONNECTION that babies and young children have; some say that newborn babies are in and out of their bodies until they make the adjustment between the physical and non-physical worlds.

There is a lovely story told by a writer known as Dan Millman in his *Warrior* books, recounting the incident of a little girl who insisted on being alone with her brother, a very young baby. Their parents, somewhat perplexed but loving, peeped in through a crack in the door. Her words were, 'Baby, tell me what God feels like. I'm starting to forget.' What a magical thing for a child to say!

Well, Rebecah also took a lot longer to forget her divine connection. There was a magical awe in her whole being which 'lay about' her for a very long time.

At a young age there followed our own little miracle! Rebecah pointed to the sky indicating, with the language we had available, that she came from, 'up there'! I fell back in a breathless wonder! Did I understand her correctly? Yet there was no mistaking her meaning. It was one of those times in life that you can't believe what you are experiencing. This was proof of everything I believed; the pre-existence of the soul and the ability that children have to carry that knowledge – so teaching us, if we'll let them.

The magic of Rebecah has ever been present. She is an angel, a dolphin and a human rolled into one. When she swam, she seemed to transform into a dolphin. Why would I receive such an image, I pondered? Perhaps it was some of life's mystery unfolding, and I knew it was only a matter of patience before I would be given further insights.

Rebecah later described the wonder and 'other-worldliness'

under the sea as everything transforming into slow motion, and said she felt a compelling urge to 'be' there.

It is not surprising then that she found herself in the ocean, as a young adult, surrounded by dolphins. They didn't actually come near enough to be touched, but close. There is, I feel absolutely certain in my heart, some kind of telepathic transfer of energy happening on a different level than the one we ordinarily perceive, allowing these times of magic to materialise. There was an invisible communication.

Seeing Rebecah as she is much of the time, with her sheer grit, determination, tenacity and capacity to endure, both mentally and physically, it is surprising to observe the angelic – almost ethereal – side of her being. Starkly contrasting though these qualities are, somehow she embodies a blend of the two and calls on both these human and angelic traits to see her through life. Those who know her, who themselves carry a keener than average sensibility, will testify to this.

Rebecah and her dolphin connection carry with them a common bond in communication. I shall endeavour to explain. In *Journey into Oneness* by Michael J Rhodes, there is a passage describing Michael's astral or dream state encounter with whales as they are dying from having been beached.

Michael speaking: 'I felt surprised and enormous sympathy.'

Dolphins communicating with Michael and his guide: 'We share a conscious knowing. As one knows, all know…'

> 'Why do you die on the beaches?' I asked.
>
> 'The reasons are physical, but the underlying cause is a movement in consciousness…'

As one beached whale was left stranded,

> Teams of people took turns to sit with it… everybody who could get near enough to help was there… The consciousness of the whale and humans was combining… It had made the decision to live.

Thank goodness for a change in human awareness, and for those with pioneering spirits who are willing to put their necks on the line, risking ridicule in bringing these things to our awareness.

The connection I am making with Rebecah is this; dolphins are not using speech when they communicate with humans, so what *are* they using? Rebecah, even now, has difficulty with language, and, like the dolphins, probably uses her other senses – particularly intuition – more than she realises, to make up for the deficit, although I am aware that dolphins also have a form of speech. Telepathy is the ability to know what someone is thinking, and if you are going to allow that, it is rather a good idea to have nothing to hide; purity of thought, don't you think? She, like the dolphins who carry the energy of 'love' in the sea, carries the frequency of 'love' on the earth, along with countless others, of course. Where are our values here?

Do we know that love binds, sustains and helps create all things; that it is the life force energy by which all that is, exists? If not this, then most of us have a sense that if we don't do things with integrity, there will be an ultimate 'backlash', and it amounts to pretty much the same thing.

Kristi Jordan wrote about her autistic daughter, Adriana, in *A Child of Eternity*. It is a compelling book that brings tears to your eyes. Adriana makes virtually no contact or emotional connection with people. Any notion that she understood language – let alone read and write it – was not outwardly demonstrable until one day when, strapped into a chair, she typed in the word 'cat' – and there was stunned amazement! Using a method called 'Facilitated Communication', Adriana carries on to demonstrate such a depth of understanding as to render the majority of us impotent. She gives us so many insights that it is difficult to know which to choose. Here are a few: 'I emanate light to other people with autism because I know many of them chose the same return as I chose'... 'I use telepathy for love'... 'I open people's hearts for God'... 'You not understand guides are trying to talk to you but you can't hear them because you interrupt them with your opinions'... 'You judge too many things'... 'Love will save the earth...' I think this little autistic girl has said it all.

Rebecah will ascertain her own life's purpose, and I'm sure there are many great things in store for her. As she left for Africa in June of last year, this poem followed in her wake.

Rebecah in Africa

Savour each moment of the now
Feel the real you as you see – allow
The depth and the joy to rise from inside you
Knowing that, to yourself be true.

Let the road rise up to meet you
Let adventure and all earth greet you
And be part of your fulfilment
Knowing you are heaven-sent.

I know you are because I can remember
At five years you pointed to your sender.
He's part of who you really are
He's part of us all, not from afar:

Enjoy, be happy, my precious jewel;
Your passion, life force is your tool
I wouldn't have you any other way
And look forward to being with you one day (soon)

You chose deafness – do you know why?
Was it so you could fly so high
Above the commonality of word
With thought unbroken – be really heard
In the strength of your own being
There for others – help their seeing?

Was it to realise your telepathy
With sharks, dolphins? ...Not apathy
Is your sure path, commitment all the way:
Vigour, strength, divinity are yours – and you don't sway.

Child of Our Time

Rebecah was born in Malaysia. The humid atmosphere, acrid odours and sound of blaring car horns contrasted with the tinkling bells of trishaw taxis and the Muslim call to prayer. These formed the background to our then familiar world. Little did we know at the time that her world wouldn't be quite like our own.

Her birth was one of the most exhilarating and miraculous experiences I have had. What followed was a little more daunting, but that excitement and wonder at the mystery of it all in those initial stages was an 'in the moment' experience unsurpassed throughout the rest of my life. I had never before experienced such love, such a desire to cocoon, protect, cherish and hold this fabulous little bundle. Indeed, to me there has never been anything so perfect and precious created. I felt so proud of myself as I gazed at her and saw the resemblance both to myself and to family, although surprisingly she was more like my father than my husband. My father was the only blond-haired, blue-eyed person among us who could transfer those genes. However, she was Stuart's and my creation, that was for sure – at least on the physical level, anyway. This was mother love at its most profound, and I knew too that I shared this feeling with those who had gone before and those who were yet to come. It was a gift common to humanity.

Rebecah was beautiful and oh so alert. I felt that I had somebody special on my hands; a little pearl in the ocean of life, sent from heaven! I noticed that she was never disturbed by noise, but if I touched the side of her cot ever so lightly, she jumped out of her skin. It didn't occur to me at the time that there was something amiss, thinking that she had grown accustomed to activity around her.

Fatimah Hospital was run by German nuns. It was clean and efficient, and the babies were dressed in beautifully designed cotton knitwear which I thought was a lovely touch. Rebecah was a long time in coming, required the use of forceps and was, to use Stuart's word, 'grey' on arrival. She was placed in a bath of warm water, where she turned pink, was shown to me quickly, and whisked off to an incubator. The bonding with me would have to be delayed a little, and I certainly wasn't going to argue. Stuart, who'd been with me throughout the birth, and very supportive, I may add, was overwhelmed by the whole procedure. As I gazed at her for the first time in that brief moment, thinking how like my father she was, I told her that she was already trouble; but my words belied my love and I knew it wouldn't be long before I could hold her in my arms. The love from the German sister in charge was enough for the two of us and the whole world in that moment. She'd been telling me off during labour, and I'd shouted back! I asked her later if she forgave me and her reply was, 'What do you think?' We both knew that she had our best interests at heart.

It didn't occur to me that the greyness represented a lack of oxygen, or that the forceps might have caused damage. Stuart was privately vigilant about observing any possible deformity and had his own ideas about the sort of decisions he thought he might have to make. I never suspected anything was seriously wrong, even though they rushed her to an incubator.

I had asked my doctor, a handsome young Indian-Chinese man named Dr Negara, for as natural a birth as possible and he did his best to comply. He himself was no stranger to tragedy, having lost his own pregnant wife in a car accident not too long before the birth of Rebecah. I surmised that this did not impair his judgement and that tragedy can often touch the soul in ways that we here on earth don't always discern. Privately, my heart went out to him, though I didn't have the maturity to say anything at that stage in my life. Our relationship, such as it was, was more on a professional basis. Perhaps someone with greater experience might have made alternative decisions or even advised me differently – who knows? – but circumstances dictated that *he* was my doctor, and whatever happened, I personally felt that it was all in 'divine order' and that Rebecah, myself, Stuart, James (our son) and all those touching her life are the richer for it.

We brought Rebecah home to a large house in a town called

Ipoh. The floors were tiled in marble and the walls were plain with the odd wall hanging here and there. We had a visiting amah who washed, and sometimes babysat. She was marvellous with Rebecah. Her name was Sarasah. From aged three months, if Rebecah fell asleep with her she'd cling on to her skirt so that Sarasah couldn't sneak away unnoticed. A clever little bundle she was turning out to be. There life continued with constant rounds of visitors and outings, and Rebecah usually accompanied us. She didn't seem to find the humidity a problem; she knew nothing else at that stage.

The days became weeks, and the weeks months. I began to notice things about Rebecah. Next door but two lived a couple, Sarjit and Manjit, with two children of their own. We have remained friends and in fact Rebecah and I revisited them not long ago. Sarjit told me that there was something 'not right' but I didn't believe him. His own child was severely impaired and I thought that he was being overly sensitive. (Sadly since writing this, Savinder, their second son, has died; but Rebecah and I were with him not long prior to his death and felt privileged for that experience. What a shining example to humanity he was!)

So, I had a child who could crawl, pick up a bottle and feed herself at the age of four months, but who never responded to sound, and in particular the sound of my voice. 'Mummy's coming' produced no momentary silence. I vividly remember going to pick her up in the mornings and she'd be lying playing, sometimes crying, but not often. As I opened the door of her bedroom, it always came as a surprise to her. I guess that this was the true time of my realisation. I wasn't admitting it. The joy and excitement on her face as her glance met mine was a moment to freeze frame and treasure, always. The joy was mutual.

As she grew a little older she became more and more excited each time she was picked up in the morning, and seemed more interested in going downstairs to see what the day would bring than being hugged and kissed by me. Some parents have told me that they felt that their child didn't want to be born. With Rebecah, this was so obviously not the case. Life has gripped her almost from day one. Everything within her environment – whether people, objects or nature – was greeted with wide-eyed enthusiasm. She continued and continues to be interested in pursuing the active and all-encompassing joys – in all the variety of forms – which this world has to offer.

Looking back at those earlier moments, I didn't fully realise what I do now, that children project the divinity of the God force they experienced before birth onto the parents. (I am assuming here the pre-existence of the soul, and Rebecah was later to provide me with evidence of this, as outlined in the opening chapter.) Of course, however meticulous we are, we let them down somewhere along the line, even if it's only delay in changing a nappy. This, sadly, is part of the human experience. I did my best. To use Sarasah's words, 'Auntie loves this baby *sooo* much. I can see it.' And it was true.

We lived in Malaysia. Rebecah, as I mentioned earlier, was blond, and remained blue-eyed and, of course, was different in physical appearance from the local children. Everywhere I went people wanted to touch her and look at her. She had a special aura that people perceived if they couldn't actually see.

There are many such children now. Some are known as 'the indigo children'. Many of them do not respond to institutionalised authority or enforced learning. I meet them every day in schools and they are here to bust the system. Some of them are psychic and can see and understand things differently from us, hence we often don't know how to teach them. We can't teach them what we don't know ourselves. Hey, we need love, creativity, harmony, trust, compassion and understanding, not enforced and sometimes meaningless learning! We need to adapt the nature and content of what we are teaching these children. More about this later.

For the uninitiated – that is to say, those not familiar with the deaf – can you imagine the challenges facing the parent of a deaf child? Do you know, for example, that an object has a mouth shape and pattern accompanied by vibration at the back of the throat which actually conveys something meaningful? Do you know how long it takes to convey this practically to a deaf child? I certainly didn't know, and it was some time before I found out. Little did I know what was in store for me.

Rebecah, now, is a shining synthesis of human endeavour. All the teachers of the deaf and their pioneering predecessors, the psychologists, the technicians who applied their skills, all those people willing to listen to their hearts and stand against convention by not calling the deaf *dumb*, or locking them away from society, all my efforts – and of course Rebecah's own efforts – all culminate in a person overflowing with the best that mankind has to offer. If life here is a game, and I suspect it is, and the negativity and limitation imposed on us with our three-dimensional form of reality can yet produce this, then I stand back in awe of the game. Seeing and knowing what has been achieved here touches my heart and gives me joy. No wonder I have been guided to write my story.

I hope you can share even just a little of that joy because we all know of life's atrocities, and wonder what it's all for. Most of us, myself included, look for answers beyond this dimension, or for some higher form of explanation as yet unreachable, unattainable, or in some form of belief system. The joy in seeing Rebecah as she is should be attributed to human effort, without needing to look elsewhere. If there is a God in all of this – and I've searched the planet and never found him – perhaps this is a new thrill for Him too. 'Let's see how impossible we can make things and still watch humans come through with flying colours!' I wonder if God is asking himself if he could achieve such wonders given the same circumstances?

I write this way at this particular point in the story because personifying God creates separation, providing space for blame and resentment. How I empathise with that feeling! But the chasm of separateness can be filled, in part, with love, and most powerful is the love for a child. I wish to express also that our own human efforts often seem to go unrecognised, unheralded and unrewarded. I'm sure that in actual fact, they don't.

This book, then, isn't just about myself and Rebecah, but about countless individuals on this awesome yet challenging planet of sorrows which we occupy. It is my greatest wish that people will see themselves and their own lives reflected through ours, and know too that their lives have not been in vain, and that the great and valiant efforts they have made will not go unrewarded, even if they appear at this stage to be unrecognised.

Rebecah's Early Years

DISCOVERING REBECAH'S DEAFNESS WAS A STUNNING BLOW, a devastating force that knocked the wind out of my wings – and I was flying high. Beauty, intelligence, an endearing personality: Rebecah had these. Even at three months old these traits were self-evident. Of that there was no doubt. Something, however, was not complete, and I knew in my heart what it was. Rebecah was four and a half months old when I decided to finally take her to the ENT (ear, nose and throat) specialist. Some of my friends thought that I had an overactive imagination, and Stuart was in their company. Others agreed that it was time to 'face the music'. (I wished it had been music we were facing!)

From the time of Rebecah's birth until aged about four and a half months, I had been struggling to come to terms with the growing suspicion that Rebecah was deaf. Not long after the birth, whilst still in the hospital, I looked along the row of newly born babies. Rebecah was easy to spot; the other babies were all Chinese! There she lay, awake, her soft, downy wisps of blond hair and her pale skin in stark comparison to the others, and her deep blue eyes gazing around, trying to make sense of the world. At that moment something profound stirred from deep within. Was something alerting me at some level?

I wondered why she was awake whilst the others slept. Did the bustle of hospital routine not impact her little life in quite the same way? I reflected on how special I thought she was, but this deep inner stirring, as yet unexplored, remained. I didn't like the idea of her being in a dormitory-style regimented room, but settled for what was the best on offer in nursing care and was grateful for that.

She herself was so very alert. Her zest and excitement for life was becoming apparent at this early stage. She wouldn't even keep still for the photos we tried to take of her not long after she was born. I seem to remember her straining to look in every direction but at the camera, and we never did get a good photo, they were always at funny angles, with skewed faces – and she was so beautiful! So that small, insignificant point bothered me, which showed my attachment to trivia! I had to wait another week, and the tranquillity of our home, before she bore testimony to my inner claims, that of being the most beautiful child ever!

There were many telltale signs along the way, indicating that she was deaf. From very early on I had attached a musical toy to the side of her cot. It had, as one might expect, absolutely no effect, so I bided my time, thinking perhaps that she was too young to respond. I didn't want it to shock her but rather to soothe her, so I'd only play it when she was awake, or perhaps beginning to drift off to sleep. Needless to say, I didn't pay much attention to this little clue.

Her basket, which was probably an old washing basket, handed down from other expatriates – for this is how things were done – rested on two chairs in the lounge and was propped against a wall. We would carry on life as normal, and she fitted in around us; or so I thought. Actually, my life was turned upside down, and I loved it. My philosophy was to get her used to noise so that we wouldn't have to tiptoe around her. I thought that my philosophy was working very well! However, if the side of her cot was touched by mistake, she'd jump and go immediately into that 'shock' mode that small babies demonstrate. I really didn't like her to do that and it upset me to see it, so I avoided it as much as possible. However, I do remember it happening on one occasion when there had been quite a lot of noise and I wasn't expecting her to react that time. That was another little mini clue. I don't remember her exact age, but it would have been around two and a half months, because I remember also thinking that the cot on the two chairs idea wasn't safe anymore, as she was becoming too active!

I began little tests, but wanted to perform them without shocking her, so I'd clap when she wasn't looking, but if she was aware of my being around anyway I couldn't be quite sure of her response. At around aged three months I began little distraction games, making noises behind her back. There was no response, but I was undaunted outwardly, and kept going with my games, periodically. By the time she was four months old, she went happily in a round baby walker on wheels, which had a small seat inside allowing her feet to touch the ground. Effectively, she was walking with the aid of this wonderful device, and it was a great frustration saver. It enabled her to reach pan cupboards and empty their contents, not to mention the freedom of the rest of the house, which was quite large by Western standards, and with marble floors. Great for baby walkers with wheels!

It was while she was in this useful device that most of the 'testing' was done. Friends of ours, Shirley and Eric, had a baby, Ben, who was only about three weeks older than Rebecah. We were in their home when both Rebecah and Ben were in their baby walkers, so I played my clapping and talking games with both of them. Ben turned every time. I mentioned this to Shirley. I was always in awe of Shirley, who was much more self-assured and capable than I was; older too, and a nurse, with considerably more 'baby' knowledge than me. She just looked at me and said, 'Oh, Ben's not deaf.' I was certain then, though I hid my anxiety. Shirley agreed with me that I should take her to the specialist. And I did.

Stuart didn't believe me, but came anyway. I'm used to him not believing me. He still doesn't and he has a few more shocks to come about a number of things. These shall remain my secret for the moment.

We found the doctor's office, tucked away in a little side street somewhere. Rebecah, oblivious to the purpose of our outing, was her usual active, bubbly self. She was dressed in a pretty cream bolero top, with embroidered edges and pink rubbers over her nappy.

We sat facing the specialist and I began to speak. I explained that our baby was deaf and began relating the reasons I thought so. Rebecah was bouncing around on my knee, trying to reach the things on the table. (Her name was Nadya at the time, and it was later that we changed it to Rebecah.) Stuart began to interject with his version of events, and I didn't really understand what he was talking about. The specialist came to my rescue and told him politely but firmly to butt out, and that I, as a mother, knew what I was talking about. This was one occasion I didn't want to be right!

There was no technical equipment. We went into a room which was set up especially for his patients. It was equipped, as I remember, with toys which made noises. His diagnosis was based on the same techniques I had used myself; that of creating noises behind her back with her being otherwise distracted. In this case I was the distracter! The moment had arrived and the testing began. Inwardly I shook, and stilled myself with a pregnant pause. There had been many such moments, leading up to this one. This gradual dawning, this slow awakening to what I knew was the truth, was finally to be confronted. No more waking up with renewed hope each morning that the whole thing was just my imagination; no more variation in the clapping games to convince myself that she had heard me.

'She is so deaf, hearing aids won't make any difference.'

Those were his words. Stuart was stunned. As we came out of the surgery we stood there looking at each other. I became detached, as if nothing had happened. In that moment I didn't feel anything.

The immediate aftermath of this incident is a complete blank in my mind, but it wasn't long before the full force of the blow struck home. My hole was deep, my depression profound, the tears flowed and I was devastated. However, what held me together was that there was something wonderful about this baby, and I knew it. Besides, there was one consolatory factor: when you've sunk as low as you can, there's only one place left to go, and that's up – albeit gradually. For a long time Rebecah's deafness felt like a long-term bereavement which became worse with time, not better. It was there to face me each morning. Happily, in later years this changed and in fact it more than changed (personally, I've changed). It did a complete about-turn, from despair to hope and a deep sense of excitement.

Unconsciously, I'd set my focus on having the 'perfect' child. This necessitated having all the faculties as we understand them, and I had imagined anything less would not be desirable and cause more suffering. Buddha was right in that we cause much of our own suffering. If I hadn't had all those ideas about how Rebecah should have been, and accepted what was, still doing my best for her, all those needless hours of despair might have been saved. Coming to terms with things would still have remained a huge challenge, but once I'd let go of the 'image', teaching her started to become exciting. This, however, was a gradual process.

I'm going to embellish this point because not only has it been an important factor in my personal growth but it has also reflected strongly in my attitude towards many things, including bringing up my children. In fact it has been a powerful happiness factor in my life. A great deal of wasted energy goes into what might be or what should be – the 'what ifs'. We give ourselves unnecessary anxiety. We then add to this our judgment and attachment to how something should look, and give ourselves more grief. A very good example of this was starkly illustrated to me in the street not long ago. A lady I was chatting to said that her daughter and partner were moving into their new home.

'How lovely,' I said.

'Oh, but I do wish they would get married first!' she replied. Her attachment to the judgment about how it should look, or perhaps what others would think, gave her suffering. Why couldn't she just enjoy what they were doing? How many of us live our lives like this? I rarely waste my energy in this way now, but instead pour love and light on to things. My children are so used to this attitude that after her seven-month trip in Africa, Rebecah told me that if a situation got a bit scary she'd just think of me and she knew she'd be safe! (Glad I didn't know… just jesting!)

And so, did I give myself a hard time? Regarding her image, she wasn't as good as other children; in her personal growth, she wouldn't have normal relationships (and some professionals later agreed with me), and so on and on. I even declined to send letters to friends with new babies thinking that they would consider me of less value if I did so.

As a baby Rebecah was alert – and I mean *alert* – and very advanced! I used to wonder if I had a child prodigy on my hands, and in fact subsequent IQ tests rated her as being the brightest deaf child in the forty years' experience of the person doing the testing at the time. I had played all those internal games, telling myself that she *did* respond to the clapping behind her back, to the click of my finger, or to my voice; but given the obvious fact that too many of the same tests would produce a curious turn of the head as she wondered what I was doing, she didn't respond! Rebecah did not respond to sound, and this was absolutely inconceivable to me. Talking to other parents of deaf children, I found mothers often had a hunch before birth that something might be amiss, some sort of a premonition; but as for myself, nothing!

She was just four and a half months old when diagnosed, and yet I'd suspected well before that – perhaps from as early as two months, and even before that I'd wondered, as I remarked earlier, why the musical toy on her cot had produced no response. Sometimes there is a fine line to take when listening to that inner voice, especially when it's seemingly negative, and I had always tried to focus on keeping thoughts positive, not giving vent to fears. As we grow on this terrestrial plane we learn to be discerning and that ability takes a long time to develop sometimes, don't you agree?

I speculated on the actual birth of Rebecah, which was long and required the use of forceps. I never felt inwardly that this was the cause of the damage, but others did. There were suggestions of suing the gynaecologist, but this was not an option for me. I wasn't into blame then, and I certainly am not into it now. There was a reason for her deafness and I intended to try and find it. Unlike many parents, I didn't feel guilt, and therefore felt no need to hit out, just sorrow. People do the best they can with their lives, and I was doing the same.

A reply to a letter I later wrote to a Tibetan lama suggested that the cause might have been forceps, and that idea has subsequently been reinforced by psychics. The baby noises she was making at nine months, according to health visitors in England, were not those of a deaf child. Later when Rebecah did acquire some speech, her voice tone was uncharacteristically lilting in the right places, and not as monotone as that of many deaf children. My psychic friend attributed this to her having heard in the womb. Being a music teacher, I listened to lots of music while carrying her, and with conscious intent that she should imbibe it at some level. Perhaps she did. God works in mysterious ways… who knows?

When I was four months pregnant, Stuart and I had a car

accident and for a moment I thought he was dead beside me. Neither of us was hurt (in fact I've always felt protected in some strange, unforeseen way), but the shock was pretty severe – and shock as we all know can create spectacular outcomes in one way or another! Could this have instigated her deafness? I believe that it did but that Rebecah chose to be born deaf, and the chemical reaction from the shock was the physical way of creating the defect. This idea, of course, has no medical foundation; it is merely a feeling, with no scientific logic.

I'd like to offer a quote that aptly describes how I feel about all this. It is from a book called *Journey into Oneness* by Michael J Rhodes:

> Understanding is not always appropriate, for it attempts to rationalise mystery. Mystery is truth unrealised, while most understanding is based on rationalisation rather than realisation.

The mystery of Rebecah's deafness is still unfolding, and in the discovery is the 'realisation' of our life's journey together. It is of no real consequence to me to know the physical reason for Rebecah's deafness, but the search for a cure (now ended), the reason why, and the ongoing pursuit of the 'correct path' has taken us on many an adventure which has brought us to where we are now.

It would be fun to explore these adventures together – to relive them, as it were – and discover in their telling what new revelations unfold.

Just prior to Rebecah being born I discovered the books of this Tibetan lama (mentioned above) under the name of Lobsang Rampa. I was never able to achieve the exercises he taught like seeing the aura, going into other dimensions astrally, or conscious astral travel (although I've had dream memories fleetingly akin to it), but the books have had a lasting and profound effect on me. The life story of this astounding man must be almost unprecedented, in our known history, though I have to say many don't believe it. His books lifted me into a whole new realm of thinking and understanding, and have been a true inspiration in my life. I wrote to this wonderful man, in the depths of my despair, asking for help with Rebecah's deafness; a cure is what I was really after, and he replied. Naturally I was overjoyed to receive a reply, but the letter didn't hold out much hope. I think perhaps in hindsight I wasn't ready to hear some of the truth. He said that the forceps at birth could well have been the cause of her deafness but, more importantly, that I would learn a lot from it. How right he was, on this second point.

Much later on in life I gave this letter, sealed and in another envelope, to a friend who wanted to brush up on her psychometry skills. She picked up that the person who wrote this was overlooking a harbour (correct), and that he felt deeply about what he was writing and wanted so much to help! This, believe it or not, was a shock. I had always unconsciously felt that whatever was my lot in life, was my lot, and I certainly didn't expect sympathy or empathy. I think you could describe the feeling as an underlying stoicism. It was probably my first real understanding that someone outside the family could love me, and was perhaps one of the first steps towards self-love.

We are not used to people in leadership positions having spiritual or empathetic dispositions, at least not in the West or the majority of countries. Priests, politicians, and figureheads who *could* do so much are sometimes even worse, so there's not a lot to aspire to in the way of role models. Tibet, before it was destroyed by the Chinese, was an exception. You only need look at the Dalai Lama and you can feel a heightened sense of consciousness emanating from the man, an aura, so to speak. In the Dalai Lama there was both a political leader and a spiritual leader.

Well, Lobsang Rampa, a high lama from Tibet, was showing genuine love and care towards me. That was quite something to experience!

Another experience I had around Rebecah involved going to a seer, which occurred while we were still living in Malaysia. I was introduced to him by a friend of ours, a devout and open-minded Hindu named Pakri Sami. On the journey there he said that I was protected whilst driving, and although this wasn't a conscious thought at this stage, I kind of knew what he meant and still feel that way. I don't remember much about what the seer told me except for two things: one, that I wasn't to wear black; and two, that Rebecah had to change her name, as the vibrations carried with her current name would not give her the right life. Her name, as I've said, was Nadya at the time. He said that the name meant 'no-yes'. Her middle name was Rebecca, and I loved that name, so it was agreed that that was to be the one, providing I changed the spelling. I dutifully did so, and am glad because Rebecah's life certainly bears testimony to his 'prognosis'.

Sound is a vibration, and energy. Any musician will tell you that the right sounds, or vibrations, must be in harmony in order to sound beautiful. We wish to carry inner as well as outer beauty, so the right name is important. I have read stories of souls before being born trying to imprint the name of their choice into the minds of their parents so that they are assured of carrying the right frequency with them to help fulfil their life's purpose. I would like to add another valuable aside here.

A couple I know, friends of mine, have a son called Dominic. They had never been interested in religion or spirituality in any form. However, one day, about two years ago, they read a book called *Conversations with God*, by Neil Donald Walsh, and asked Dominic to have a look at the book too. Dominic was six at the time, and very bright. He quickly scanned the pages and his reply astounded his mum and dad. He told them that he didn't need to read this, but that they did, and that on the planet where he came from, Planet Latin, the information in this book was common knowledge. He added that oneness and love was their reality. When asked why he came to earth, he told them that God told him, though God was not a man, more of a knowing inside, and that what Jesus Christ had started he had come to help finish. Sheffield, where they still live, was where he had to be – and then the rest would be taken care of.

This is the quality of many of our children, and we need to take the time and the patience to find out what they're all about. It often requires of us that we break into new paradigms of thinking, moving away from convention or belief systems; being less controlling and more of a friend. My nephew, Thomas, who is classed as remedial, further exemplifies the point I'm attempting to illustrate. Anybody who knows Thomas would find this a joke, and yet in terms of standard school requirements, he is. His mother, Sue, says that she knows he thinks in three-D.

We are evolving quickly, and our children are showing us the way, if we'll let them.

Home

HOME IN ENGLAND CALLED US WHEN REBECAH WAS AGED nine months. Rebecah was already walking, and in fact had been from aged eight and a half months. The long plane journey to England was something of an ordeal, as she did not like being confined and cried much of the time. England, at that point, was in my heart, but I was making the journey alone; Stuart was to follow later.

During the previous two to three months I had become somewhat depressed and very thin. Life in Malaysia had begun to feel oppressive. I couldn't go for walks as it was too hot and humid and there were no pavements. Driving places felt too risky as the Chinese attitude to death was fatalistic, and I never knew if I was going to meet someone on the wrong side of the road when cornering a bend. The social merry-go-rounds with the English were proving tiresome and I wanted to meet people of like mind.

Many were beginning to ask me about what were, to me, more interesting matters, like esoteric material and life after death, and so on, which was a real boost; but mine was only book knowledge and I said so. Most importantly, I needed urgently to get Rebecah home! In England there would be a structure around dealing with deaf children, and although I always knew that I would feel the need to make my own decisions, they had to be informed ones. Finally, I simply wished to share Rebecah with my parents, knowing that they would appreciate her and see the depth in her that I saw, and they did!

Stuart's mother had come out to visit us in Malaysia and she had been very sensible with Rebecah. She would regularly nurse her to sleep and give me a few quiet tips, like putting a tiny drop of brandy in her milk; but there's nothing like your own mum – and certainly nothing like mine! On the love front, for children and grandchildren, there was and is 100 % unconditional loving and giving. Both my parents were simply ecstatic and overjoyed with Rebecah, perhaps even all the more so because she was deaf. They felt, as I did, the need to help; to 'be of service'. Their reaction to her combined with my own to expand more than times three the love I felt. I would do anything in my power to see that this little girl was given every conceivable opportunity to grow and excel as a human being. My God, she would do this! How could I not help to bring to fruition such depth of character, such zest for life, such grit and determination and such connectedness to the God force within? This meant growing myself, in order to be of help, and it meant learning from Rebecah in ways I shall relay as the story unfolds.

There is perhaps an inherent trait among most humans to 'be of service' – to feel that what you do with your time somehow serves others. It gives meaning and purpose to what we do, and can justify any zest for money, power or status. The irony is that we do not wish to become involved with helping people if it doesn't interest us, or if it's not the work for which we are paid. We become afraid of being 'sucked in'. Possibly this is because we have to balance our life's purpose with serving others and earning a living, and we instinctively know that people might drain us if we let them. We also have to balance that which we love to do, for it is here that our best service is given, to ourselves and therefore to others. I understand these things.

Many people, as time went on, didn't want involvement with Rebecah, and I could understand this, but thought that it was their loss. I truly believed that it was their loss, and still feel that way. It is an honour and a privilege to know Rebecah, as many people would tell you if you were to ask them. Some of the people around me were a bit shallow, but then they found me too deep. So be it.

We quickly became acquainted with the education system with regards to Rebecah and discovered the many admirable people within it. There then began another painful episode in becoming familiar with the development and education of deaf children, and one or two more shocks.

Having contacted the authorities, our first port of call was with an audiologist, Dr Ivan Tucker, whose practice was in a large hospital in Manchester. (Little did we know at the time that we would encounter Dr Tucker later in life in a very different capacity.) An audiogram was produced on the basis of tests given. These tests consisted of loud sounds played through a large set of earphones. The sounds were monitored both in pitch and decibels. They were so loud that they would damage the eardrums of a hearing person. Response to these sounds (and with a young child of ten months, reactions necessitated careful observation), would determine the hearing loss, and subsequently, the type of hearing aid required, and possibly have some sway on the type of education advised, though there were other factors involved here. I always felt that the tests were primitive and could potentially damage any residual hearing. Nevertheless, I had to subscribe to the system and let it go.

I do however remember Dr Tucker's words, which were that she was a 'normal little girl' who 'happens to be deaf'. When all the emotions are heightened, the words of specialists are very potent, and those dealing with new parents of handicapped offspring need to be cognisant of this. It was a lovely gesture, to make light of her handicap and see her as normal; but it belied the work involved in ensuring that the 'normality' continued.

For example, young deaf children can play happily around hearing children, as their play runs more or less upon parallel lines and language has little impact. In this respect, as a parent one can be forgiven for being lulled into a sense of 'normalcy'. This changes considerably as time goes on. Deaf children do not meet the language requirements of their peers and social gaps naturally occur. Most parents in my experience were interested in their children excelling above others, or being 'brought on' by other children, particularly academically. There may have been some empathy, but it wouldn't have stood up to any tests if it were detrimental to what they perceived to be the progress of their own children. Any attempts to integrate Rebecah into the same class within school – and often even socially – were met with no more than thinly disguised compassion. In the classroom, their fears were well founded as Rebecah would have held them back were they to go at her pace, and without assistance from a teacher of the deaf; but socially their lives could have been so much richer if they'd made the effort. Often they didn't, but some did and I thank them. More about this later.

I was instructed by the authorities to make contact with an advisor for the deaf, one who gave advice to parents of pre-school deaf children. By this time we had moved to our own home in Cardiff, and it being a capital city, we were very well placed with regard to facilities for the hearing impaired. People living in the country areas would have to travel in to Cardiff, or adapt to existing facilities, which might have been less than adequate. Having said that, I really wanted to bury my head in the sand somewhat and didn't want to make 'contact' only to be told the worst. I rebelled internally, although actually knew that it was the best thing to do.

My child was very precious to me. When other people get hold of our children, they begin putting them into categories of, for example, behaviour patterns, intelligence brackets, or in my case, response to language patterns, and there were many more to come. However well intentioned the professional, things become depersonalised. It is their job to make these assessments, and in all honesty, I can't think of a way round it, but knowing that didn't help matters. And it was to get worse. Rebecah became more and more 'defined' as she got older, and it used to hurt. It gave me acute inner emotional pain.

It might be worth relating a couple of stories pertinent to Rebecah being 'assessed', as many parents have to undergo similar types of issues with regard to their children. Indeed, most of us have to undergo these debilitating or degrading experiences, with a visit to the doctor or an interview for a job, to provide but two examples. The first one took place when Rebecah was about four years old, and we had already moved to Durham. Our 'advisor' had obviously looked at her audiogram and decided that she should be in a school for profoundly deaf children and not a PHU (partially hearing unit) attached to a mainstream primary school. This necessitated lengthy daily travel or boarding. Boarding at four years old would have happened over my dead body! I didn't put it to him in those terms, needless to say. It was more a case of her perhaps being a little young.

He delighted in telling us that she was a typical profoundly deaf child. I roared and seethed inside on hearing that one! What he was really saying was, 'I know. I'm experienced.' I attempted, in vain, to put my side of the story to him. This was, as already stated, that at four years old I felt she was too young to board, and that she still needed my input and love, every day, and that the other school he was suggesting would have been too much of a cultural and social shock to her. It was, quite frankly, in quite a rough area and the children were taught 'Makaton' sign language, which was similar to BSL. I didn't know this sign language very well. Not being able to communicate with my own daughter didn't sound like a very good option for me.

He did not like me for having my own opinions, and called me 'a very awkward woman'. Subsequent dealings with this man became difficult, to say the least, and he also made life rather awkward for Stuart and myself. He did, however, admit to us later that Rebecah was very bright. I remember him saying when Rebecah was much older and we had successfully got her into Mary Hare, which was – and is – a grammar school for the deaf, 'I do my job, Mrs Taylor, whatever you may think.'

The second incident I would like to share was, by contrast, on more of a personal rather than a professional basis. I was visiting an aunt who was actually dying of cancer. I loved this lady a lot and cried buckets when she finally died, and I certainly wasn't going to do anything to upset her. Rebecah could be heard outside the bedroom window as she lay and I sat with her, talking. I can't remember the exact words, but she said that all Rebecah's traits and speech were just like those of a deaf person she knew, and she went on and on as if to plug the point. I didn't read any malice into her comments, but did wonder why she went on so much. I was gutted.

Did this mean that all the modern methods of teaching were no improvement on the old? Did it mean that all my efforts, which were ultimately aimed at integrating her into the hearing world, were futile? I held back the tears, swallowed the emotion and, as on so many occasions, kept it locked inside me. I never saw the lesson in this little episode. I never saw it then and I don't see it now.

Currently Rebecah's demeanour is very normal, except when she speaks, or signs (when she uses the facial expressions that are part of signing), or is trying to lip-read in difficult circumstances.

Maybe somebody somewhere can tell me what that was all about, but fortunately it was a very minor incident and therefore relatively easy to let go of. The thing is, it was poignant to me at the time because as someone approaches death, we imagine a hitherto untapped wisdom coming from that person. This is obviously not necessarily the case. Sadly, and somewhat ironically, my aunt's grandchild, Rachel, who was not born until after her death, is very handicapped, and I have just been discussing with her mum all the things I have been writing here, and how so many of our experiences are identical. Liz, Rachel's mum said, 'Oh, write them, write them!'

To continue my story, when Carol Jones, the advisor to parents like me, walked through the door of our Cardiff home, my indignation was assuaged and I liked her. She was a great comfort to me too, as I never made friends with the Welsh mums very easily, but Carol seemed so normal. As for any resistance I had, it vanished, returned and vanished again. One thing was for certain; I needed her professional expertise, and as is often the way, I was something of a support to her, as she was going through a rather painful divorce at the time.

Rebecah had already been fitted with powerful body-worn hearing aids, as subscribed in accordance with her audiogram, consisting of those which carried AA batteries within metal cases, and which had wires leading up to the aid itself. I used to sew matching pockets for them, but whichever way you looked at it, they were not aesthetically endearing; neither were they inconspicuous. If that wasn't bad enough, they seemed to make no difference whatsoever. It was then that I learned a few facts.

The first pair of hearing aids had arrived in the post whilst we were living temporarily with my parents. Stuart fitted them and Rebecah, surprisingly, didn't object. I thought they were ugly and primitive. I have photos of her with them on, with a brown woollen holster to hold them on her chest. As they seemed useless, once again, I bided my time.

Later, Carol, the advisor, explained that Rebecah would have to be trained to use them. From Rebecah's audiogram, which, as stated earlier, measured both frequency and decibel loss, Rebecah was diagnosed profoundly deaf. Somehow, from the audiogram, it was possible to reverse the process and let hearing people hear what Rebecah and others like her with a similar loss could hear with the hearing aids on. Carol brought a demonstration tape for me. I listened and was shocked. This was another of those 'diagnostic' moments which was to prove most painful!

Speech was totally unintelligible. It was not possible to discriminate between any of the sounds. In fact, the only discerning factor was the amount of syllables in a fuzzy buzz. I cried. Carol went home and apparently cried too. She knew I wanted her to leave and not return, and she told me that I could only bury my head in the sand for so long. She was right, of course. Carol questioned her own professional decisions and wondered if she had been too brutal too soon, but I had demanded the information and once again there was no blame on my part.

Carol was an excellent teacher. We discussed all the issues surrounding deaf children and, of course, the role of the parent – i.e. myself – and how draining that was. Leaving no stone unturned, and with her careful guidance, I became Rebecah's teacher.

As Carol explained there were and still are many contentious issues around total communication, i.e. signing and lip-reading combined as opposed to the pure oral (speech) and aural (listening) and lip-reading approach. This second method was the one I was trying to teach Rebecah. I was hearing, so this smacked of normality to me. (It is interesting that nine out of ten deaf children are born to hearing parents, so there remains this conflict of signing verses speaking.)

The 'aural' side of the process meant utilising what little 'listening' skills Rebecah had, with the aid of hearing aids. The response was, as stated, nil at first, then gradual, for reasons which I shall endeavour to explain. It is impossible to amplify any consonant to 100 db at the frequency of speech without losing it. If you think about any consonant, it is preceded by a soft bit, i.e. 'n' 'p' 'l' and then by a vowel sound, which serves to elongate the consonant. The soft bit at the front, which determines the consonant itself, becomes lost when amplified to the level required, and there are some children with absolutely no residual hearing whatsoever, and later in life many of them refuse to wear hearing aids at all.

Added to this was the fact that Rebecah had virtually no hearing at the frequency of speech, and so any input she did have, minus the consonants, was vowel sounds, which also become distorted with amplification. There wasn't much hope of acquiring language at this stage, was there? Now let's compound the issues a bit further. Rebecah didn't know that she was supposed to make a noise at the back of her throat in order to respond. Indeed, she didn't know that she *had* to respond!

The whole performance was carried out in order to exchange ideas, convey intent, express emotion and all the other things we use language for. At this stage, what we could swap was a series of gestures, including hugs and facial expressions and a lot of 'doing'. We would make cakes together, hang the washing out together, play tea parties, go to the park and much more. All the time I would be trying to explain things. We would both have to stop what we were doing to look at each other, while I made these futile gestures with my mouth. Everything took at least twice as long and was exhausting for me. Rebecah was always obedient, stopped what she was doing and tried to understand. Her obedience astounded me, and inwardly I applauded her for it, particularly as much of my 'mouthing' was meaningless to her. She continued to be 'obedient', and continues to be this day, bless her. (Nowadays, she tells me off if I'm not concentrating!)

I listened to Carol, who was balanced about everything and knew well what was going on. She taught me how to teach Rebecah using a method of lip-reading, voice production and 'listening'. There was a skill in catching Rebecah's attention, speaking close enough to the microphone in her hearing aids, to make use of what little auditory input she could utilise, and using words that were both lip-readable and meaningful.

But first Rebecah needed to understand that what I was doing *meant* something, because it was a long time before she made the connection between an object and what I was doing with my lips; in fact it took months. The word I worked on the most was the word 'hot'. I didn't want her to burn herself, so it was a warning as well as a feeling, when near the heat. The warning or pleasant feeling also depended on the facial expression, an imperative factor in the teaching of deaf children. Another reason that this was a good word was that the lip pattern for such a word is visible, that is to say at the front of mouth. A word like 'ink', for example, would be almost impossible to lip-read because the vowel sound, 'i', and the consonant 'k' are not visible on the lips or in the mouth shape, at all; 'i' (the same applies to 'ee'), has no particular mouth shape, and 'k' is produced at the back of the throat.

This is not meant to be an instruction booklet on the teaching of deaf children, but it is quite interesting to examine the activities involved. It gives us an insight into the challenges, both in the teaching of the deaf and in the acquisition of language as a deaf person, especially one who is born deaf. So, to continue with my story once again, I finally struck gold and Rebecah produced her first sound with the lip shape of 'o' when pointing to the fire.

How she learned to vocalise at the back of her throat is a mystery. If I remember correctly, I did put her hands on my throat from time to time so that she could feel the vibration, but whatever the reason, the connection was made and the first hurdle jumped. Carol said that it was a very good sound and at a natural pitch. I was pleased, and thought to myself, *You aint seen nothin' yet!* It had taken about six months of repeating this word thirty to forty times a day before gaining a response! I also used the word 'car' to keep her occupied whilst driving, and although I knew that 'c' was a non-runner, I thought she'd get the idea. She didn't!

Can you imagine the joy? When did my son (sixteen months younger) learn to talk in all of this? I honestly don't remember. What I do remember is him coming out with a sentence one day and being amazed, feeling guilty at the lack of attention I'd given him, but of course, delighted. It made me realise that hearing children will learn to talk anyway, whereas deaf children will not without the necessary input.

And so to return once more to Rebecah and the word 'hot'. The 'h' sound and the 't' sound didn't come until much later, when we'd played many games with consonants; the vowels were learnt largely by copying lip patterns. The sorts of games we played with consonants were blowing a feather with a ‘p’ sound, which formed the basis of differentiating between ‘p’ and ‘b’, which look the same on the lips. All this was very well, but it wasn’t doing very much for our communication system. It was far too slow for a bright child who needed to simply tell me what she wanted and understand what we were doing. Rebecah was getting frustrated and so was I.

Improving my Skills

THE NEXT MOVE WAS TO IMPROVE AND SPEED UP OUR communication skills. Carol had been very patient and allowed me to pursue my chosen method of communication, but it was far too slow. Rebecah was gradually responding to the hearing aids, as for example, when I called her name when she had her back to me, she would turn. It was the amount of syllables that gave her the clue, as she would turn if I said, 'Samantha', but it was a start.

Carol suggested a sign method known as Paget Gorman, as this method of communication was grammatically sound whereas BSL (British Sign Language) wasn't. This appealed to my sense of logic too, so I began lessons and quickly passed on my new-found knowledge to Rebecah. Much of what I used was a very literal representation of the meaning of the words I was teaching. For example, the word 'in' was represented by a fisted hand turned sideways with the index finger of the other hand going inside.

For other signs I would point to something then sign it. At the same time I was using the spoken word, trying to ensure that she could see both my actions and lips at the same time. I have to admit that I bent the rules and made up my own signs, too.

Books were a very useful tool in our education process. I spent many hours looking for books with pictures that were sequential so that the story was self-evident. If the story told itself through pictures, the words I was using would serve to support already forming concepts and would therefore be more easily understood and subsequently reinforced. I could also, at this stage, expand our language with the use of more expressive vocabulary, adding adjectives or verbs to our story: 'the crocodile "snapped" (complete with gesture) his jaws together, and he was frightened (complete with gesture).' I would then have to remember to keep creating situations in which to use these words, but it was fun. (I also remember making a crocodile from egg boxes and playing games with it.)

From being a very young child, possibly as early as ten months, I used books with pictures and words during my play sessions with Rebecah. A picture of sweeties would, for example, be accompanied with a mime of us eating them and I would then point to the word. We did this so often that when I covered up the picture and pointed to the word, accompanied by the spoken word, 'What?' and an expression of bewilderment on my face, Rebecah would mime the sign for the word. She was experiencing word recognition from less than a year old. Don't ask me what good this did. Probably none at all, but it was, again, fun! Rebecah seemed to enjoy it, which was part of the deal. More than anything I wanted Rebecah to be happy and her learning had to be enjoyable as well as informative. The happiness factor was a big deal with me, and I often allowed her to do things that perhaps she shouldn't have done.

These book sessions, then, occupied much of our time together, but the selection process meant that I couldn't always choose the most interesting or exciting stories. The emphasis, as described above, was more on discovering appropriate illustrations, and those which would in effect tell the story by themselves, without the use of language. The stories needed to be simple enough for me to be able to explain what was going on. I would often have to resort to action or mime, to keep them interesting. Too much language with abstract detail would not only have lost her interest, but would also have been wasted effort! Too much fantasy would require language she didn't have at all, and would have been confusing. For these reasons I omitted nursery rhymes, which were often macabre or just a series of events without being a real story. The idea of a rhyme, e.g. 'I do not like green eggs and ham, Sam I am,' would have had no effect on Rebecah, neither would an accompanying song.

As the point in all our exercises was the acquisition of language, if I didn't keep things exciting and meaningful, she wouldn't have given me the attention, resulting in less learning. Later in life Rebecah felt embarrassed at not knowing nursery rhymes or some of the more famous children's stories like *Winnie the Pooh*, and promptly set herself the task of learning or reading some of them. Her friends, who'd been brought up with sign language, did learn them, as their language was natural, just like ours! (Once again, there'll be more about this later.)

I feel it appropriate to add a little aside here. *Winnie the Pooh* contains subtle nuances of language which are appreciated by an older child. Without these nuances, the stories are not so interesting, and so it was never the right time to tell them to Rebecah, or at least that was my experience. She enjoys them now, however. I was able to savour their delights with James, and we spent many a happy bedtime together. What joy I had when he was able to laugh with me as that 'ragged' balloon went in and out of the very 'useful' pot!

The explanation of abstract things, and concepts such as the past or future, were even more of a challenge. Picture this: with a normal hearing child, language has been assimilated gradually during babyhood. Information is taken in through the ears and somehow interpreted within the brain in a meaningful way, and this is an ongoing process until the chid can master its body enough for speech to develop. This is not happening with a deaf chid. Language and the translation of words to convey something are not happening. Watching lip patterns with no sound is also meaningless.

Gradually, Rebecah understood that every object had a name, but 'past' and 'present' was much more of a challenge. To overcome this I used a sign for food at each meal time. Breakfast was signed 'food', and then I pointed to the top of my lower arm. Lunch was signed, 'food' with a point to my middle arm and dinner, 'food' and my wrist. Bedtime was indicated with a point to the underside of my fingers, and then I would indicate an obvious sign for sleep. This was, closed eyes, head on one side and two prayer-like hands at the side of the tilted head. The future would be indicated as starting out from the fingers of an outstretched arm and moving away from it with my other hand.

Slowly the connection was made between how many sleeps into the future or how many in the past (away from the body behind the shoulder). This, then, became my time line. I would often have to try to mime events, as language was too limited to describe them. If, for example, we were going to the swings, I would use the future time line, point in the direction of the park, then mime 'swings' till Rebecah got the idea. My logic was that if I kept using the same method, she would get the idea of things that were about to happen, when they were less obvious, and I couldn't give a directional sign, as for example the direction of the park.

Certain key words – especially verbs, such as the word 'remember' – became essential to our vocabulary, and I used them often, accompanied with a sign and a mimed incident that I knew she would remember, so that all our conversations contained a point of reference. Once again, she would slowly come to understand the word, as in this case, 'remember', so that I could use it in other contexts and we would extend our vocabulary together in this way. For a long time, I knew every word in this vocabulary of hers, and any stranger trying to talk to her stood no chance.

If you or I were to learn a foreign language, we would translate what we were learning into a language we could already understand; this would be our point of reference until the language had become sufficiently familiar to us that we could think in it. A deaf chid has no such point of reference.

What does a deaf child think? Does it have non-linguistically conceptualised thoughts? To put it more simply, does it have thoughts without words? Probably the answer is yes, but eventually these are replaced with language. Rebecah tells me that she doesn't remember having thoughts without language. A deaf child has virtually no language. Does this slow down the development of a deaf child? Yes. Does it cause the child to cut off from the world? Yes. Does it cause much frustration? Yes. Are their social skills hampered through lack of interaction with their peers? Yes. Is their information input severely restricted creating immaturity and naivety? Yes. The list is endless and the mountain too big to climb, yet climb it we did, right to the top of the highest peak and down the other side!

This is due by and large to the education system and the generosity of social services in this country. I think we are very lucky, and I give my heartfelt thanks to all those who have worked and pioneered to create a system whereby deaf children can climb to the top of whichever mountain they choose, and yet can also help those who struggle. I would, however, like to add another of my little asides. I don't hear many people saying, 'Thank you'. So much has been achieved with regard to the deaf of this country. Deaf awareness, as with many other things, has grown enormously over the last few years; in fact, along with computer technology, human rights, stress awareness, mobile phones, profound messages in films, and more, it has grown almost disproportionately in the last few years, and this is a delightful scenario. However, saying thank you is so rarely done; and yet giving thanks and praise enhances that which you have, does it not?

School

WE LIVED IN CARDIFF, WALES. HERE, FROM THE AGE OF TWO, Rebecah attended a marvellous school for the deaf, or hearing impaired, to be more politically correct. It was an aural/oral primary school. By aural/oral, I mean limited listening with hearing aids, (aural) spoken language, using the voice (oral) and lip-reading; no signing.

Stuart and I were invited to the school for a Christmas pantomime. It was our first 'taste' of deaf children en masse. Goodness, what a shock! The children came on stage, complete with costume and innocent enthusiasm. Each delivered their own line, whilst, placed nicely to one side, stationary, was a boy holding a tall piece of card with their lines written clearly in large, bold print. This was fortunate. I couldn't recognise a word they were saying!

> Christmas is coming, the geese are getting fat,
> Please put a penny in the old man's hat.

The first line was delivered in a squeaky high voice, the second like an imitation of a giant, (not intentional). Both were unintelligible. Have you ever laughed and cried simultaneously? I did that evening. I couldn't believe that my daughter was about to be included in such a rabble. Surely she was above this! I am being totally honest about my thoughts here, but please understand that these thoughts were not without compassion and appreciation for the efforts and achievement of both staff and children within this school.

I could imagine, at this stage, having a preview of a future life, looking down from heaven. In heaven, everything is idyllic, and we don't know stress or anguish in any form, let's say – 'Pretending' – as I would later say to Rebecah. Now, as all the details of this life unfold on our imaginary cinema screen, I recoil in horror at what I must face and want nothing to do with it. To give another analogy, I'm a metal, being mercilessly tortured in the furnace in order to become steel; shining, pure, strong and enduring! Did I really have to put Rebecah through all this? The answer was clearly yes.

The headmistress was obviously very proud of the performance and what it reflected. She was coming from a place of a 'passionate desire'. She wished to help these children succeed, and I both liked and admired her for what she did and who she was. She was not, however, coming from a place of being constantly emotionally challenged, or to be more frank about it, traumatised. (I am not comparing this to the obvious extreme traumas to which mankind is subjected, in all their varying forms, but it is important to recognise and acknowledge trauma, because being unrecognised or undetected it can lead to greater problems.) This was *my* domain and the domain of all the other parents. The teachers would have their traumas in other areas of life. I think it's safe to say that none of us escape.

The classes were small, consisting of about six children to one teacher – who, incidentally, had to work very hard! Often the children would sit in a semicircle, sometimes with radio microphones worn over their ears, which connected them either to each other, or the teacher, or both, whilst the children 'talked' about interesting things or played games. All the time their eyes had to be glued to the teacher, who had to be engaging as well as informative, or their attention would stray.

Every week each parent brought in a new toy, at a cost of fifty pence. There was much in the way of descriptive language, not to mention the excitement, at opening each carefully wrapped little gift, which the children got to keep and take home at the end of the day. Stuart told me that the things that in some way moved provided the most fun, and I was sure he was right. The search for this toy provided me with another pleasurable task each week. Anything that was geared to helping Rebecah was where my energies lay.

It was a good school, and on reflection I was very lucky to be able to take Rebecah there. The staff were kind and caring, and the atmosphere was warm and friendly.

I remember taking my father for a visit. We sat together at the back of the hall whilst assembly was taking place. We were the centre of attention and provided good opportunities for discussion and language. On that particular morning, the school had changed its routine, and all the children sat in a different direction. Rebecah had been in the school for a couple of weeks or so by that time. She was just two and a half years old, but that didn't deter her. Apparently all the school were wrong. As they sat one way, she sat facing the other way – the way she had grown accustomed to sitting previously – and gestured for everyone else in the school to do the same. We all laughed.

Another little incident is worth pointing out. Upon viewing the rest of the school during my preliminary visit, I was taken, as one might expect, to see what the older children were doing in the other classrooms. One class was discussing age and how, with each year, we added another year on to our age. There were obvious difficulties with this even with nine- to ten-year-olds. In order to assist with the abstraction of a 'year', the teachers had equated this with the measurable growth in their height. As they got older, so they got taller. The teacher turned to me, then asked the children to guess my age. I am very tall so, as you can guess, I was approximately one hundred!

And so Rebecah was deaf, and there was no point in pretending otherwise. I'd gone through two depressed periods, one in Malaysia when I wrote to my Tibetan lama, and two when Carol Jones had played that tape. It was now time to accept the situation and wholeheartedly throw myself into whatever needed to be done. It required total surrender and the letting go of any resistance I had about what things were supposed to look like, whatever ideals I might have had, and dedicating myself to the task in hand. I'm glad I did because hanging on to illusion just gets more painful, rather like wearing a pair of tight shoes that you think look good, but which cripple you. What a relief when you take them off, and an even greater relief when you realise you don't ever need to wear them again! It was at this point that the excitement of the challenge began to set in.

My attitude began to change and therefore the task in hand took on a new perspective. Each task, each bit of new ground covered, became rewarding, not only for the results, but also for the inventive mechanisms around creating the desired outcome. Manjit had told me once that handicapped children brought so much more joy, as nothing was taken for granted. These enlightened words were starting to be true for me.

An achieving child certainly can give pleasure, but if things are taken for granted, the pleasure diminishes and can even turn to anger if expectations are not met. This is not an expansive feeling. I like to feel expanded. I like to feel that whilst there's that ever-present goal, that pot of gold at the end of the rainbow, the *process* also becomes part of the goal, and then there are many little rainbows and pots on the way. If I don't look around in each moment to enjoy them, then I will miss them!

James has benefited from this wisdom. I left him to develop at his own rate, enjoying him, without pressure, just intervening when I thought it was necessary. In fact I thought, as he was growing up, that he would do something with his hands, like joinery, or engineering. Whatever James wanted was fine with me. He was always a lovely boy, and that was the best! In his most recent interview, he told me that for the first time, it was who he was that got him the job. He said that it was his whole ethos on life that shone through, and it was for that reason he felt proud of his achievement. I too felt proud, but I have to say in all honesty, that both his being and his achievements have exceeded my expectations, not that I ever really had any, as I always left things open-ended.

Soon after Rebecah had begun the Cardiff school I met the mother of a deaf boy who had reached secondary age. She was telling me that he was in a normal school and was coping, but something belied her words. I didn't believe her and was later told that the boy was not coping and was very miserable. I wanted Rebecah to be happy. If she had been able to cope with a normal school with added support (and she wouldn't), the social interaction and peer group camaraderie would have been missing, and what would have been the point in that? Early school suited Rebecah as she enjoyed the perpetual activity and social exchange. I didn't feel too badly about her attending so young as she did seem to enjoy it. Cardiff was, however, short-lived, and Stuart's change of job meant a change of home and town. James and Rebecah were about two and three years old respectively when we moved to county Durham.

The task of finding a school for Rebecah was pretty awesome. I visited Newcastle School for the Deaf and I have to say I felt a sense of foreboding as the oppressive Victorian building began to enshroud me. The staff, as ever in these schools, would jump through hoops to help these children. Unfortunately, they were short-staffed for Rebecah's age group, and there were far too many children within a fairly large age span for one teacher. It was an impossible situation. I dare say if I'd hung on in there, things might have changed. I wasn't going to find out.

We scanned the area, including Northumberland, which had been recommended to us by the Cardiff headmistress. The county were offering a mainstream school with a twice-weekly visiting peripatetic teacher for the deaf. I was assured that this was a marvellous approach and that Rebecah would be well catered for. The class teacher was to wear a phonic ear (a radio microphone, linked directly into Rebecah's).

I did some investigation and managed to speak to the lady who would become Rebecah's teacher at the start of the term. As I suspected she knew nothing of phonic ears or deaf children. I am a teacher myself. I am, though not officially qualified, a teacher of the deaf. I believe my vast experience with Rebecah entitles me to this honorary title! The teacher in question, with the best will in the world, would not have been able to cope. I knew far too much of what would be involved, and so it was another impossible scenario. The search continued.

To cut a long story short, we eventually settled on a partially hearing unit attached to a mainstream school. It was a modern school, light and airy, with a happy atmosphere, and only a small group of children within the unit. What's more, there was a nursery assistant, who although officially unqualified as a teacher of the deaf, had become most adept at handling the children, so in effect they had two teachers, which doubled the ratio. Excellent!

There began my introduction and ensuing lasting friendship with her new teacher, Vivien Crawford. On a preliminary visit to the school I left Rebecah in her capable hands, while Stuart and I pursued more incidental matters like somewhere to live. She was, as Vivien later pointed out, quite rebellious for a three-year-old. She squeezed the hands of fellow pupils rather too tightly, and refused to be supervised when being escorted to the toilet. I didn't always recognise Rebecah's reactions to her insecurities, and learnt of things like this too late. Perhaps it was better that I didn't know, as she, like everyone else, had to learn to deal with life's little lessons.

Unlike many teachers of the deaf, Vivien was not especially ebullient or 'in your face', as it were (rather like I am), but had a fairly quiet approach, requiring the listener to focus on what she was saying. Apart from being a lovely person there was something refreshing and liberating about Vivien, and I trusted her implicitly. Some judged her a little harshly for her approach, but those people failed to look below the surface. She was so utterly astute and had the capabilities of every child sussed. She knew, for example, if a child wasn't coping with the oral approach and needed sign language. This didn't always go down well with parents, or advisors who disapproved of signing, but she was proved absolutely correct. She was correct in her assessment – both current and future – of Rebecah, too.

It was Vivien who first explained to me the real implications of the use of sign language. I had already learned that deaf children growing up in a household with deaf parents fluent in signing acquired language earlier, and that this was often reflected in a greater ability in written language later on. It was obviously quicker than the oral/lip-reading approach, and cut out much of the ambiguity (caused by failure to lip-read) and frustration. I could probably have saved myself heartache and arduous effort if I'd known and believed this at the time, but there was always the concern that if I didn't teach Rebecah to speak when she was young, she might never have learnt or what she did learn might have remained unintelligible. I at least wished her the best that she could achieve. I owed her that.

What Vivien explained was that as long as the children had a language, transferring to the written word, and possibly the spoken word, too, was far less of a problem than you might imagine.

Rebecah spent five happy years in this school, four of them with Vivien, who provided an excellent foundation for her, in more ways than one. Rebecah was happy with Vivien, in that unit. She felt secure and loved. Vivien had a policy of, 'Do not let the sun go down on your wrath,' so Rebecah always returned from school in a happy state of mind with any bits of 'naughtiness' forgiven.

When able, she accompanied Rebecah in joining mainstream classes for maths. Here Rebecah did very well indeed, but maths is a relatively non-linguistic subject. The whole idea of having a partially hearing unit attached to a mainstream school was to enable integration, but the emphasis was on being partially hearing. (Rebecah wasn't partially hearing but profoundly deaf, and theoretically should not have been in that unit.) Thus, integration, for practical reasons, rarely happened. It is not difficult to see why. Vivien fought her corner hard, but other teachers were, according to her, somewhat dismissive of the unit, which rather left her and the other unit teacher out on a limb. Even if the teachers had been educated in the issues concerning hearing-impaired children it would have been difficult to integrate them. I am fully aware of both sides of the coin.

This situation resulted in Rebecah and the other children in the unit playing almost exclusively by themselves. Even James didn't play with her very much at school, naturally gravitating towards his own peer group. Socially, at home, and up to about the age of ten, Rebecah integrated naturally with the children in the street, who were accustomed to her, and this included two Marks, who were really James's friends, both of whom had time for Rebecah, even as she grew older. Their mums did too, and I'm grateful to them for their thoughtfulness and compassion.

Whilst on the subject, there was another friend, Kath, who used to bend over backwards for Rebecah, and who used to observe her wherever she could. She used to give me little anecdotes that she'd picked up from other hearing children, like 'She can always do it' when it came to sport or athletics where Rebecah excelled. If Rebecah was with a group of hearing children en masse and the teacher or instructor didn't know she was deaf, Rebecah would watch intently, and if heads had to be lowered she'd keep surreptitiously lifting her head so as not to make any mistakes. Kath noticed all these things. Thank you, Kath, and the two Marks and their mums, Alex and Ena. I needed people like you to keep my faith in human nature.

However, not understanding the spoken word had become part of Rebecah's experience. There were certain situations in which Rebecah understood things, as when with me, or her daddy, and at school. In other situations she had to learn to adapt in order to fit in and this became the norm for her.

This leads me back to the subject of Vivien and her signing. I understood that a child growing up with sign language as a first language would quickly learn that there were many situations where he or she couldn't use it and would make the necessary adjustments, just as Rebecah had done. But I still wasn't fully convinced by Vivien's earlier argument, that of signing being more easily transferable to written and/or spoken language.

Because BSL (British Sign Language) was developed primarily by the deaf, to serve their needs, grammar, syntax, and often past and future tenses were ignored. I figured that if I used a sign language that was grammatically sound, then Rebecah's English would be sound also. This certainly did not follow. She ignored prepositions and pronouns, as they were meaningless to her and the development of a time line, my own invention, or so I thought, provided for our pasts and futures. All the signs I used that were meaningful to her would have been just as meaningful in BSL; including the time line. Using BSL would have had the added advantage that other people could have used it with her and not just me, as was the case with the sign language I was using. She would, however, have had to attend a school which used sign language. There were none in the area.

At this point I would like to add a few pertinent and valuable little asides, not directly related to school. Here they are.

Not all hearing impaired children develop speech. Sometimes, especially in wholly deaf families, there is a conscious choice not to, as it is deemed unnecessary. There is a general tendency for those with the best hearing to have the best speech and vice versa. Rebecah tells me that she doesn't see a difference in the quality of speech when comparing friends from purely aural/oral schools where signing is not officially used, and from total communication schools where signing has been used all the time.

I think that Rebecah might be being politically correct in saying this and that statistics may indicate the contrary, but any parent wishing to make a decision on these matters can examine what is available for themselves.

A person who has become deaf has a different set of problems with which to deal. Beethoven had already internalised sound, so with his extraordinary ability he was still able to compose, though he probably went through hell. Evelyn Glenny, the percussionist, went deaf at about twelve. She interprets sound through the body and has normal speech. Both are nothing short of miraculous! Jack Ashley, the MP, is a credit to himself and us, but if one listens to him, there are noticeable traits of loss of intonation and clarity in articulating. However, none of these people were born profoundly deaf, and all had acquired language.

Advantages of Deafness

REBECAH, AS I SAID, TOOK A LOT LONGER TO FORGET HER divine connection. Perhaps that was because she didn't hear the rubbish that we all involuntarily pick up around us through conversation and the media.

There is a collective consciousness, which nearly all of us reflect to some degree or another, and most of it is fear based. We worry for our safety, health, having enough money, whether people are awful to us, and so on ad infinitum. People carry with them their own belief systems, opinions and rigidities, which keep them locked into a limited sphere of existence and can add to the feeling of being separate from one another.

Rebecah wasn't imbibing all these things, at least on a conscious level. She grew up knowing nothing of snobbery, class distinction, accents, politics, racial hatred, and very little in the way of fear-based thinking. She didn't even develop much fear around physical danger, and I certainly didn't consciously provide her with any of those fears. I won't say she was totally devoid of it, but generally I was aware of the refreshing innocence she carried and potential for a closeness to compassionate and open-minded values.

When Rebecah was little, and I will be honest and say that I do not remember her exact age as it has merged with the recall process, I tried to explain to her that she came from my tummy. Somehow she understood. I wanted her to grow up with as much understanding of life as I was able to give her and not be the butt of jokes through ignorance. She understood, which was amazing to me, and then that little miracle followed, as described in the opening chapter. I remember the actual incident vividly. She stood, swinging her leg from side to side whilst leaning against the arm of my chair.

She continued the conversation by indicating, through signs, that before this time she came from 'up there' and pointed to the sky! As I described earlier, I fell back in a breathless wonder!

Naturally I wanted to know more, but language of the celestial nature was not in our vocabulary. She was unable to embellish the subject and, sadly for me, I had to drop it. I think the memory remained with her because she didn't have the usual distractions described above.

Having briefly touched on birth, I needed her to understand the concept of death before experiencing it – or was it the other way round? I can't remember. Once again that 'time' thing is indefinable. The sign for death would mean nothing without the concept. The most obvious way to explain it was to sign sleep and never waking up. But even that was dodgy, to say nothing of life-after-death concepts.

I was staying with my parents-in-law when the perfect opportunity arose. I picked up a well illustrated book, *Bambi*. Rebecah was still very young, possibly not yet three, because I had vague memories of James still being able to sleep in his pram, but I could be wrong. I told the story and she was fully attentive, but I didn't actually believe that she was taking everything in. How wrong I was. We arrived at the part, inevitably, where Bambi's mother had died. I explained the death as that of being asleep and not waking up. I described and 'actioned' some shooting, thinking that she might have observed this on TV at some point, and that it might reinforce the idea of death. The absence of the mother with Bambi in the illustrations, and the fact that Bambi was obviously now growing up, were all helpful indicators.

However, I was doubtful about whether I could convey the concept. I acted sad, shook my head, signed and Rebecah stared back, seemingly emotionless. I looked once more at the book, pondering on how I could add bits here and there and turned again to look at Rebecah. Tears were streaming down her face! I was in awe of this little girl. She had understood! I then had to explain that it was only a story…

It seemed to me then that Rebecah, and therefore all children, was and were born with a certain conceptual understanding that we as adults don't understand or perhaps don't even think about.

Rebecah seemed to have a remarkable sense of knowing about

things, not only in other-wordly aspects, but also in her knowledge of practical things, which seemed to defy all logic. Simple or detailed explanations where practical language was involved would often leave her baffled, but she would know distances and directions, for example, which belied her years. Alternatively, things that one would expect to be obvious to her were not, and vice versa. These two parallel levels yet remain, and although the gap has been bridged, they are still a feature of her being. Even I fall prey to her indignance if I pitch it wrongly.

As a very little girl, I remember trying to give her a choice between two drinks, and try as I might, I couldn't make her understand. She would, however, take you to the park, or notice if you'd painted the room a different colour. As an adult, she might debate, for example, how the discrepancies between the cultural facets of being an American and being British might affect the life of a traveller. She would know the geography involved, too. She might not, however, have encountered the fact that people from the southern states speak entirely differently from those further north. Thus in an in-depth discussion it would appear as a discrepancy, baffling the uninitiated listener.

However, as the heading of this particular chapter suggests, we are talking here of the advantages of deafness. Why would such a gap in levels of understanding be an advantage, one might ask? For the astute listener, the opportunity arises for empathy. The realisation of such a gap exposes the struggle of the deaf person, and how we take so much for granted. This produces within us, if we are sensitive, a humbling quality, and we need 'humble'. Humbleness, or humility, is another one of humanity's saving graces.

A recently acquired American friend of mine, Renee, said that she thought Rebecah was simply amazing. She added that she felt so 'humbled' in her presence. Whilst sitting in the car with Rebecah and 'grandma' she watched as Rebecah drove up to the front door, helped her grandma inside the house and departed with an, 'I love you, Grandma.' And yet another notch was grooved on the ladder of life; another step along the road to inner awareness, as Rebecah unconsciously removed the barriers in another and freed them to see that little bit further. (Downs

Syndrome children have this effect on me. Do they do that with you? If not, go and meet them.)

During my days of learning Paget Gorman, the headmaster said that one of the boys came up to him and physically shook him, saying, 'You never told me you could hear the rain!'

The headmaster's shame was expressed, 'I am so, so sorry.'

Even professionals get it wrong!

Dolphins seem to have an affinity with children and the handicapped. I wonder, do they know something we don't? I will tell you a true story, or at least, true as it was told to me. I met a man in London who claimed to be able to communicate telepathically with whales and dolphins. He was in a Sea World type of place, in Canada, where a white beluga whale had been caught and was on display, so to speak. He immediately began to pray for its soul, but the whale interrupted with – and I can remember his exact words, '*What are you doing?*'

The whale, he said, went on to explain (telepathically, of course) that it had allowed itself to be caught, otherwise it wouldn't have been there, and that when children came in, it would perform its antics, and when there were just adults, it wouldn't. If he didn't believe the whale, he was just to hang around and watch.

Needless, to say, he did watch, and as you might guess, when the children came in the whale jumped, flipped, and all the rest. You name it. When there were just adults, it floated around, doing nothing in particular. Rebecah has an affinity, like countless others, with whales and dolphins. In the water, swimming with dolphins, she is not disadvantaged. Underwater, everyone else has to learn sign language!

One of her most memorable times, as she will recount, occurred at the end of a stint in Belize, whilst with Operation Raleigh. She was on an island and all the equipment had been packed up and the Raleighers were waiting to leave. They had nothing to do, so Rebecah suggested to a few of them that they explore the island. In one area they discovered it was sinking and had dropped below sea level, so of course they had to swim to reach the other side. Rebecah had to leave her hearing aid, at least, the one that was still intact, on a tree, and remember exactly which tree, so she was a little behind the others but caught them up. Halfway across they found themselves surrounded by dolphins. The dolphins, as stated in the opening chapter, never came quite near enough to be touched. The young people felt elated and greatly privileged, and of course desperately wanted to feel and stroke them but were 'teased', out of reach.

Another memorable occasion was our time spent together in a healing sanctuary in Glastonbury. We were enjoying a mother/daughter 'rebirthing' session in a sauna-sized pool. While undergoing the experience, I saw, in my mind's eye, this huge whale once again, filling the pool with a presence of love and knowingness. I felt the whale was Rebecah, of course. The man conducting the session seemed to think that there was some sort of healing needing to take place, concerning a deep-seated or subconscious resentment around the birth of Rebecah and the resulting (if it was a result) deafness. Nothing came up for either of us. However, awareness of the whale's presence was very real, and without Rebecah I wouldn't have had the experience.

It is difficult for the deaf to undergo these guided meditations for obvious reasons. They can't close their eyes while listening, and any lip-reading requires intense concentration, the opposite of meditation. Also, the language used may not be in their vocabulary. Rebecah doesn't know the sign for consciousness, and neither do I.

And yet paradoxically, many deaf people – Rebecah included – can 'turn off' the sound around them, and not become easily distracted by things, so easing their powers of concentration. In fact they often choose not to be involved with conversation around them, with hearing people, preferring to enjoy each other. They have a closeness, in view of their mutual dependency, and this takes them across many bridges.

James recently attended a football tournament involving deaf people almost exclusively. He commented on the good naturedness they all enjoyed together which continued in the pub after the matches, win or lose. Such camaraderie is seldom experienced, especially in sport, where there is often underlying jealousy or resentment.

Returning to our Glastonbury experience, the people running

the sanctuary were a little unorthodox and claimed to have seen us both on Sirius together, in past lives, Rebecah as a dolphin, myself as humanoid, and that we agreed all that time ago to be mother and daughter in this life. How's about that for stretching credibility and expanding thought processes? They also claimed that Rebecah was from the Deva realms; that is to say, the fairy, angelic realms, and had, unusually, decided to make the transfer to being human. Perhaps this is possible, but I have also had glimpses of Rebecah in past lives, very much as a human, and even then, I can't be sure how much of this is my imagination. But I do know this: my journey in life would be that much less rich if I ruled out such possibilities. Being open-minded is so much more fun. Thank you again, Rebecah.

Living with Rebecah has taught me to look well below the surface when seeing people. When Rebecah was old enough to make her own choice of friends, she would sometimes choose people I wouldn't have chosen, and I soon learnt to look more through her eyes and learned a lot from it. I am grateful to you, Rebecah, for opening me up and showing me things about people that I really, really needed to learn.

Isis, the woman in the sanctuary, described Rebecah's past existence as a fairy. Rebecah is tall and well built, so this has its funny side, rather like a production of *Iolanthe* by Gilbert and Sullivan that I once saw, where the 'fairy' was portrayed by a thirteen-stone middle-aged woman who sat on a flower! However, I do possess two photographs of Rebecah with what appear to be fairies on them, which I shall try to reproduce in printing. Whether or not they actually are is not clear. There is also one with a gnome taken at the same time, and although Rebecah is not actually in the photograph, she was around at the time. We didn't see the fairies or gnome whilst taking the photos, but only noticed them after the film had been developed.

There were other extraordinary qualities around Rebecah's ability to observe and understand situations, which made me wonder who the teacher was in our relationship. These were probably born out of the necessity to observe, as she couldn't rely on language.

I was very forgetful, and Rebecah would follow me around,

picking up my car keys or handbag from as early as two years of age. If she hadn't picked them up, she'd know where they were. I remember setting off from a friend's house one day and looking around for my handbag. I turned around and there was Rebecah, outstretched arms, with my bag hanging from her tiny little hands. She wasn't looking for praise – she was barely two years old, and such attention-seeking tactics were beyond the realms of her innocent mind – but was just behaving in a caring and loving way. It was natural to her to be thus.

I used to do practical household things slowly, with Rebecah by my side, always taking the opportunity to explain and thereby put language into her with every task. If I was making a cake, she would know which ingredients came next, and on one occasion, how many ounces of flour were required.

She'd watched me change the water of the goldfish many times and decided to do it herself one day, unbeknown to me. She came running into the lounge. 'Wish, wish' accompanied the sign for fish. It was said with some anxiety, as she took my hand to lead me into the kitchen. 'Wish seep' accompanied the sign for sleep. She'd only used the water from the hot tap! This was a valuable experience in understanding death, though I didn't feel it appropriate to use it as an example with verbal explanations, but preferred to let it stand, as it was allowing Rebecah to take from it whatever was needed at the time. Naturally I didn't tell her off; I knew that she was sorry.

Imagine lying in your mother's arms as a baby with her making silent lip patterns in your face. The only things you would be sensitive to would be the emotions behind the facial expressions and the general level of love and care, including, of course, the physical contact. Add to this the possibility that your mother may not know you are deaf, and that you may not know you're deaf. There's a huge lack of connection going on here and, certainly in Rebecah's case, and as stated earlier, it is not even to this day fully bridged in the way it is with a hearing person. But, at the risk of repeating myself, just a couple more examples might make us all smile – and how lovely it is to do that!

Stuart was buying her a dress for her birthday in Newbury

town centre when Rebecah was still at Mary Hare. The one Rebecah wanted was out of stock in her size. The assistant said that they had been so popular, that they had 'flown out the door'. Rebecah looked towards the door, temporarily in amazement. Stuart laughed. On holiday in Portugal, not long ago, we asked Rebecah to count the cards before we started to play. She did, and we asked her, 'Did you count the cards?'

'Yes,' was her matter-of-fact reply. Towards the end of the game someone noticed we were a card short.

'We thought you counted the cards.'

'I did,' was her reply.

'How many where there?'

'Fifty-one!'

I remember a neighbour of mine saying that she wouldn't like to have swapped her situation for mine with regard to Rebecah, and I thought to myself, how little she understood. For the most part, Rebecah was a joy to be around; every small hurdle jumped bringing such a sense of achievement. Once again, I remember my friend Manjit, from Malaysia, saying that people didn't understand the joys of bringing up a handicapped child. Sadly, her boy died not long ago, but I bet she wouldn't have swapped him, or exchanged her life with him for that of another. He was a treasure, too! He never bemoaned his lot or felt sorry for himself.

Truth

WHEN REBECAH WAS VERY LITTLE I WANTED HER TO EXPERIENCE the magic and wonder of Christmas and not miss out on the excitement of Father Christmas appearing in the skies on a sleigh, pulled by a reindeer delivering presents. It was a 'lie' in which I had decided to indulge and went to great lengths to do so. Explaining this in speech and sign language took some time and many repeated exercises, but I did it and she got the message. Needless to say, the evenings leading up to Christmas, when Rebecah was aged nearly three, were spent running to the window peering up to the skies. Her face was a wonder to behold, being alight with an awe of innocent expectation. I thought that she had held this belief for a long time, as she didn't really challenge me on it until aged about twelve. In actual fact, she secretly knew the truth from eight years old.

Later in life, she asked me most pointedly and somewhat accusingly why I had deliberately lied about this. I remember it distinctly. It was during her university years and we were on a train together. The repetitive background noise accompanied my explanation. Happily, she concluded that she would have done the same for her children.

And yet this small incident had far reaching implications, spreading out like a meshed thread work within the interconnectedness of life's tapestry. I never lost an opportunity to point out anything to do with 'Christmas', so if there were lights I'd sign and say 'lights' and 'Christmas'. The sign and spoken word for 'Christmas' accompanied everything to do with Christmas until she got the message. These conversations took place at any time and anywhere. They were 'in the moment' happenings, where opportunities could not be lost. One such moment was in the middle of the market place, where someone was watching me, and that someone later proposed that the local Round Table invest in phonic ears (radio microphones) for young deaf children and their mothers. 'You were ages explaining things,' I remember him saying in a meeting.

And so, as the topic of phonic ears was explained during a ladies' circle meeting, many people got to know of the issues facing deaf children. The main advantage of wearing them for Rebecah was that I could connect with her from a distance. The disadvantages were that she couldn't tell what I was saying and that they were rather cumbersome, especially when riding bicycles or climbing trees. They were more useful when used in a mainstream classroom situation with partially hearing children who could understand the spoken word, with amplification, so that if the teacher turned, or was difficult to lip-read, the subject would still be understood. (As a teacher, I have used them many times myself.)

The notion of signing didn't end there. My ardency at the whole Christmas saga continued at school when parents of other deaf children within the PHU were watching me also. Signing was not officially allowed here, much to the distress of Vivien, as partially deaf children were supposed to speak. In point of fact, the unit was a melting pot of children with various degrees of hearing loss and/or learning difficulties, which poor Vivien had to sort out. What amazed certain onlookers was Rebecah's level of understanding. How did she achieve such a level? This went on, once again, unbeknown to myself. Vivien was quick to point out that it was the use of sign language that escalated such understanding.

Alas, not everyone took from that experience what they might have done, and with seemingly dire consequences; but that is a story which I would need to tell sparingly, lest it cause much hurt. Suffice to say that one young person, profoundly deaf, like Rebecah, and with hearing parents, wasn't taught signing at the insistence of the mother, who, I've since been told, was watching me at that moment, and who, I'm also given to understand, commented later on Rebecah's level of understanding; and this young girl, now grown up, hasn't as yet learned to speak or relate to others easily.

Vivien quietly pointed this out to me at the time, saying that if she wasn't taught sign language soon, the consequences would be dire. The authorities and her mother fought Vivien all the way and won, but indeed, lost! The girl was later whisked away to an aural school where the difficulty compounded itself. Eventually, after much had been lost, she was whisked away again to a separate part of the school and taught sign language; but there was little interaction with the peers she had previously known and this must have created one trauma after another. There is time now for her current situation to change and I'm sure it can, God willing. I know that Rebecah is doing what she can to help this young lady and will continue to do so. We don't see the overall picture so we're not in a position to judge. In my present state of consciousness, I am deeply sad about it.

In my youthful, ego-filled state, I was happy when Rebecah did 'better' than other children. What utter nonsense I now perceive this to be! How lovely is the thought that we may all become as fulfilled as possible; the best that we can be – however that may look. Perhaps some of us are here just to learn peace, surrender, simplicity and harmony. Who knows, who can tell, who can judge?

Looking at the heading of this chapter, 'Truth', caused me to reflect upon the word and its meaning. During my time with Rebecah, especially when she was young, so many different people wanted to force their version of the 'truth' onto me.

One day, whilst I was visiting the PHU, I met a woman who insisted that deaf children shouldn't use their hands, and so Rebecah had to stand as if in a straightjacket when speaking to her. I'm sure she'd have given Rebecah a straightjacket too, if she could. I'd have liked to have given her one, extending upwards around her mouth! I can't remember the woman's official capacity in the teaching deaf world, but she didn't have much contact with Rebecah, thank goodness, or we might just have come to blows. Whether this attitude fell into the category of pre-Victorian or medieval nun, I can't quite decide. It was certainly cruel.

Then there were the signers verses the oral auralists. The headmistress of Rebecah's first school, that lovely lady again, once arranged a meeting where she wanted me to explain at length why I signed to Rebecah, the upshot of it being that I shouldn't. Another teacher told me that I mustn't teach her the alphabet. I had it displayed like a border around the room, with lively pictures for each letter, and we would sometimes talk about the different ones before she went to sleep. I wasn't hung up about whether she got it or not.

One day, Vivien called me into school to explain that Rebecah needed new hearing aids. Her body-worn hearing aids, given out at that time to most profoundly deaf children because of the more direct link between the voice and the microphone on the chest area, were, in her opinion, to be superseded by post aural aids. These, as the name suggests, were connected by a tube to the ear moulds, with the microphone behind the ear. This was not only more cosmetically appealing, but less cumbersome. Had Rebecah noticed these on other children, she might have objected to wearing her own. Up till now, she had been particularly good about it and only thrown them in the bath once, at the age of two!

I dutifully took Rebecah to the audiologist to request a pair, but was told that I needed to be referred to the ear, nose and throat specialist for his recommendation, via my GP. This was a long-winded process, but I finally made it to the ENT specialist's office. Innocently and politely I explained my situation, saying that it was really the ENT specialist that I needed, but the audiologist, and didn't wish to take up his time unnecessarily. He began asking me detailed questions about the birth of Rebecah, and I was baffled. Once again I painstakingly explained that I wasn't here about ascertaining my daughter's deafness, which was established, but it was just post-aural hearing aids I needed and that the audiologist could arrange for those. The only thing I needed from him was his recommendation.

Well, he hit the roof! He was Indian, and his English had, shall we say, yet to be perfected. He'd certainly got the wrong end of the stick. The response went something like this: 'You no want to see me you get out. You want to go London, you get out!'

The words were not exactly whispered. I burst into tears and it didn't go unnoticed! Nursing staff tried to calm me down with offers of cups of tea. Not long afterwards I was visited in my home by a social worker. Word had spread, and it wasn't long before Rebecah acquired a pair if post-aural hearing aids.

The social worker and his wife became my friends too, and visited me for an 'uplift'. Through them I learned much. They were very impressed by the fact that I had taught Rebecah sign language, although it was the wrong type of sign language, in their opinion, and wanted me to write about that. If I'd taken everyone's judgements on board I would have been one confused lady, but as Vivien later pointed out, I was always balanced about things and whatever my approach, Rebecah would have been okay because of this factor. You can see how grateful I was for Vivien's words of wisdom.

Then there was an advisor who, as previously stated, wished me to send Rebecah to boarding school, aged five, because she was profoundly deaf and should attend a school with profoundly deaf children, and not a partially hearing unit attached to a primary school. Boarding school at five years old? All these people had a vested interest in persuading me of their truths. That is what validated their lives and gave them the impetus to keep going. We all do this to some degree or another.

But I do remember the words of one female teacher of the deaf. It wasn't so much her words as the energetic exchange we shared. She just looked at me and said, 'It doesn't matter.' I knew what she meant. It took the edge off that intense seriousness about 'getting it right', and I think perhaps I've carried some of that with me all my life, since that time. Like many young parents in a similar position, when a handicapped child is first diagnosed so much energy goes into the 'miracle cure'. I even joined a Buddhist group that chanted – anything to find a cure. I took her for acupuncture, which involved hours of travelling, subjecting all the family – James, Stuart and my parents – to immense inconvenience. The truth was that Rebecah was deaf, and that was fine… it was absolutely fine!

Growing Up and Education

RETURNING ONCE AGAIN TO MY STORY, THE UNIT IN COUNTY Durham had provided Rebecah with a sound and happy start to life. As she reflects now, much of her time was spent with one boy, David, because they communicated well and felt comfortable together. I knew, however, that this was coming to a natural end and that she needed more experience at social skills and peer group friendships for her development as a person. This she wasn't getting with the others in the unit, or with hearing children, other than her friends in the street, and even those relationships were beginning to suffer a little. The next step was to get her into a school for the deaf, which would fill in these deficits. Boston Spa wasn't too far away, and it was the next obvious choice. There was considerable red tape involved, but we were eventually successful in our endeavour.

Our first visit to Boston Spa School, a huge Victorian building with a forbidding atmosphere, was daunting and yet exciting. I was too trusting of the nuns, some of whom were lovely, and some of whom were not. The teachers had the best interests of the children at heart, and the care staff with Rebecah appeared to be just that – very caring. The children each had their own lounges and dormitory areas, and Rebecah, being naturally inquisitive and active, seemed to enjoy all the activities and friendships, which were quick to formulate. Boarding was weekly, and I wouldn't have had it any other way.

When Rebecah first attended the school aged eight and a half, we visited her regularly, even going down the day after we had left her for the first time. Phooey to this false notion that children need to be hardened. They need to be loved, and demonstrably so. I had tried with all my ability to prepare her for boarding school, but as Rebecah tells me now, she was very confused. I remember the head teacher telling us that all the children had a reaction to being taken away from home. She was right.

This was to be Rebecah's. Stuart used to drop in at the school even more regularly than me, on his travels. One day Rebecah apparently broke down in tears after his departure, which, incidentally, always saddened him too. 'Daddy is very hungry,' she said to one of the kind nuns.

'I don't think Daddy is very hungry. I think you miss Daddy,' was the nun's reply.

Rebecah cried and was comforted. I didn't want my child to attend boarding school and have to be wrenched from home, but this really was the best option. Friends in the street would still play with Rebecah, and liked her, but had she not developed interactive social skills with the attendant language, those friendships too would disappear. As it was they were becoming thinner on the ground as their language grew more and more sophisticated.

Having said this, it always came as a surprise to me how Rebecah too could be choosy and wouldn't play with children she didn't like, even if that child liked her. Neither would she play with her younger cousins if there were children of her own age. Victimhood was not in Rebecah's field of experience.

The English public school system, including convents (and Boston Spa was convent in part), has in the past stripped children of love and hardened them to the point where real feeling is stifled in order for them to survive. It was, and perhaps still is, cruel. I remember a vicar friend of mine criticising me for visiting Rebecah so often, saying that what I was doing was like planting a seed and pulling it out the next day. What utter nonsense! He was a product of that system, and to me his whole life demonstrated it. And so I was wary, but perhaps not wary enough.

Quality of speech was an important feature in the schools Rebecah had attended, and I was grateful for all the efforts of the teachers and speech therapists. Many deaf children had learnt to make a noise by breathing at the back of the throat till they felt a vibration and they sort of superimposed the lip patterns simultaneously to form speech. The result was often a far-back monotone breathy sound. To understand them meant 'tuning in' and lip-reading them at the same time. The quality of Rebecah's sound was quite good and she seemed to understand me when I tried to get her to lower her pitch, and later, to drop her tone slightly at the end of sentences. Any efforts I had made were certainly reinforced at Boston Spa, where individual speech therapy sessions in mirrored rooms took great priority.

The school used musical sessions to enhance speech rhythms too, and the children seemed to thoroughly enjoy this. The staff were wildly enthusiastic about any new venture that could be of benefit to the children and this contributed to a oneness of spirit. However, this oneness had something of the nature of a double-edged sword, and at times I was uneasy.

One day, I was in the school during meal times and a nun was telling a child off, after which she turned to me with sweetness and light and began a conversation which I can't at this stage recall. She left, and Rebecah turned to me saying, 'She's nice to you, Mum, but to the children she's really horrible.'

I looked at her somewhat disbelievingly, but was to find further evidence of this kind of behaviour myself at a later date, involving another nun. Children who've now left the school will confirm such stories. Revelation of these things is not sour grapes on my part. Truth about life needs to be revealed if we are to progress spiritually. I have a friend who went to the convent here in my local town who reports similar stories of unnecessary and severe harshness bordering on cruelty. Secrets are only secrets if we have something to hide!

On a happier note, Rebecah's language and speech progressed admirably. She learnt to play cards, talk about clothes and fashion, play sport – particularly netball – and loved gymnastics and swimming. One of my highlights was seeing her play the central part as a ballerina in a mimed school play (Rebecah had attended ballet classes as a young child). A nun afterwards approached me, commenting on how beautiful she looked, to which I replied, 'Beauty is only skin-deep.'

'Oh, it is a lot more than skin-deep with Rebecah.'

I heartily concurred, of course, but was so glad that one of the 'kinder' nuns recognised it.

Many of the friendships Rebecah made at Boston Spa School have lasted. They tend to do that with the deaf anyway. Today, keeping contact is part of what is known as 'deaf culture'. If the friendships are not close one-to-one relationships, they will always cross paths at social venues or when hunting for jobs, as often the same line of work is pursued.

Rebecah was with us at weekends and school holidays. There were times during these occasions when she would sound like a monkey, especially when she was excited. I remember her trying to explain arguments with James to me, or detailed descriptions of stories she'd read, or watched on TV, and often I didn't understand. Sometimes I dismissed her too easily, and I'm now so sorry. Forgive me, Rebecah, and I must take full responsibility and forgive myself! However, I never despaired. In fact I never lost my faith in her magic and knew that it would be more than all right in the end. I held that energetic magic goalpost for her and never let it fall – and I mean, *never* let it fall! Actually, the deed is not yet complete, and I still hold it, though I've handed over my responsibility.

While Rebecah was growing up, I spent hours explaining things, teaching her, and later trying to instil grammar into her. The last venture, the grammar part, was pretty much a waste of time on my part, and I was a little too harsh at times. The sessions often ended in tears and I was not proud of myself. I think now that the focus on language was too much and she lost that bright sparkle of spontaneity and general knowingness that she had about everything. For example, we used to take her regularly on a long drive to visit an acupuncturist who thought he could help her with her deafness. Rebecah was very young but seemed to know the way there at an age when that would have been almost impossible. Later on in her life, when we first arrived at Mary Hare School ready for her to start there as a pupil, aged twelve, I remember asking her how many miles she thought the journey was and she didn't have a clue.

There is something I would dearly like to relate which will perhaps convey to the reader the arduous effort required in the acquisition of language. I feel that in telling this next little anecdote much will be accomplished by way of understanding and added interest, as it encapsulates something not hitherto expressed.

As was often the case, I had to choose when to extend Rebecah's vocabulary and when to let things go. Rebecah was still at Boston Spa School and therefore twelve years or younger, when I introduced the word 'appreciate'.

I forget the actual context in which I used the word, but to appreciate something meant that Rebecah realised it was good. She may have liked it, or may have hated it, however. She may have been grateful, or perhaps should have been grateful, but wasn't. On the other hand, it could have conveyed the understanding of something, the 'realisation'. However, it could also have meant 'gone up in value'. Without going into the grammar, we know that this word connects many seemingly unrelated concepts with the same essence of meaning. It was a word I decided to pursue in order to fill many gaps in understanding, which the reader may like to 'appreciate' for herself. I think I achieved my aim. I notice now, when Rebecah uses the word with naturalness and ease, and congratulate myself that perhaps I did get something right!

However, all this brought it home to me that there was a price to pay for the acquisition of language, and Rebecah was paying. That hard focus on language and time spent acquiring it hadn't left time for being present and alive in each moment with that lively, spontaneous zest for life. It was like a grinding down of the spirit. By the time Rebecah was aged about eleven, that extreme brightness and alertness she possessed wasn't as easily transferable to her written work which the headmistress at Boston Spa School was eager to point out. I think she took it personally that I was transferring Rebecah to Mary Hare.

Boston Spa had some absolutely wonderful teachers with excellent methods of teaching. Once again, I am grateful to them. Here Rebecah learnt such techniques as phrases spoken in rainbow patterns, allowing for the natural fluidity of spoken language. Mistakes were not considered 'wrong' but rather, weren't reinforced. There were, however, certain reservations on my part, which I won't detail here, but the time was right for her to move on. I knew this intuitively.

Mary Hare

GETTING REBECAH INTO MARY HARE ONCE MORE INVOLVED a lot of red tape. The senior child psychologist was involved, as well as the advisor to the deaf, that 'wonderful friend' of mine. The psychologist was extremely helpful and supportive, and it was thanks to her that everything went so smoothly. In view of the high financial costs, appeals had to be made to local authorities, and proof shown that this was a necessary step. Pure desire on the parents' behalf was not a good enough reason. However, the new Education Act's promotion of parental choice where possible did help. These schools were very expensive; somewhere in the region of eighteen thousand pounds per year.

The children at Mary Hare were all very bright. They had to pass two exams to get in, one academic and the other social, which involved two trips. Mary Hare is in Berkshire, and we were still living in county Durham, so the travelling distance was not much short of three hundred miles. Having passed the first half we now awaited the results of the second and confirmation of her place. Rebecah made it. I remember receiving the letter of acceptance. The language was quite complex for an eleven-year-old deaf girl.

'Have I got in, Dad?'

'Yes, Rebecah,' was Stuart's joyful and warm reply.

We were so proud. She would certainly reach her full potential here, socially, academically and in the many aspects that go to make a person whole. I soon learned that the children in her year group were like soul mates, and I knew without a doubt that I'd made the right decision. We may work our decisions out logically, but really they are guided from an inner knowing. I had kept Rebecah back a year, so that she was twelve on entry, not eleven, and never really knew why I felt it necessary to do that. It wasn't until some time later that I realised how I had been guided once again from that mysterious source; my higher self. Here Rebecah blossomed.

The buildings of Mary Hare School comprised of a distinguished old manor house with of course many outbuildings, and the setting was in huge grounds with some splendid old trees and woods nearby. Parents like us were able to rent a cottage situated among the rhododendron bushes within the grounds themselves, and overlooking the woods on the other side of the road. I was later to experience strange phenomena in those woods. It was all very exciting.

The school didn't have the forbidding atmosphere of Boston Spa, possibly because it didn't have a long history of religiosity and the attendant nefarious goings-on often found in those places. Such activities, even if they are not sinister but just overly strict, spread out somehow in their energy field and become imbibed into the building itself.

Mary Hare was, to me, a happy school with a healthy attitude. The boys and girls mixed openly and freely. Teachers on the whole were dedicated and, as was to be expected, classes were small. And – surprise, surprise – the new head teacher was the audiologist we had met in Manchester, Dr Ivan Tucker! He was an excellent choice for the school, being both strict and fair and very hard working. People liked him, and so did I.

Here there was a work ethic, yet a freedom. The children were taught to have their own bank accounts and be independent but there were sensible safety rules. And there were rules which Rebecah disobeyed.

Rebecah not only enjoyed sports but was able to develop organisational skills in her various roles as captain. She took part in many outdoor pursuits. I had always encouraged her to do this, as I knew amongst other things that it was a powerful antidote to loneliness. One child in particular comes to mind as I write these words. I can still picture her sobbing, alone at weekends, when outdoor activities had been forbidden by her parents and she had nothing to look forward to after the long academic week: no home; no activities! I found the attitude of her parents unbelievable!

Nicely in time for Rebecah and her peers, the new sixth form block was completed. The children shared only two to a room, but Rebecah, as deputy head girl, had her own. Finally, in the upper sixth, Rebecah had a single en suite room, as is fitting for the Head Girl!

I remember her closing speech on Speech Day, in front of all the staff donned in their degree gowns, and of course, with parents and dignitaries also in attendance. It was a 'grand' occasion. I made a comment to a member of staff that I'd like to be in a position to video this, as it was a day I'd been waiting for for seventeen years. Ever since her first primary school in Wales when the headmistress had leaned over to me and said, 'Rebecah is a candidate for Mary Hare,' I knew what she meant, even though I'd never heard of Mary Hare, and I knew too that she would be Head Girl. The teacher I'd dared to share that with said that she was very moved!

On to College

ON LEAVING SCHOOL, REBECAH TOOK AN EXTRA YEAR TO complete an arts foundation course and lived at home. This was a valuable year for her in learning to cope with the hearing world once again, as home provided an added sanctuary. She had learned to drive and took my car out on a daily basis.

Passing her driving test was tense but lessons were hilarious at times. She first took lessons whilst in the sixth form at Mary Hare. The instructor was used to handling Mary Hare students and had become quite adept at coping with the awkward situations. Unfortunately, Rebecah failed at her first attempt and took a second course here at home. Needless to say, mum got roped in, didn't she! As I tell the stories to friends, Rebecah goes, 'Mummy, oh Mummy, no!' and proceeds to burst into fits of laughter.

Not hearing the finely tuned revs when negotiating clutch and accelerator meant that starts tended to be a bit juddery. Hill starts were even more juddery, and hill starts at traffic lights were 'juderier' than ever! During one of our outings we were on a slight incline whilst waiting for traffic lights. After the lights had turned red for a third time and the traffic had piled up to bring the town to a halt, redemption came. She made it on the fourth attempt! As for two fingers, it could have meant twenty miles an hour, second gear, or that other thing! By the time she'd looked at me for an explanation we were on the kerb. 'No, look ahead, Rebecah!' Oops, wrong gear!

Finally she became a competent driver, thank goodness. No accidents! College was quite enjoyable for her. She tended on the whole to do way out, 'zappy' things, art-wise. However, she did some delightful pieces of work, too, and I had one of them framed as part of her Christmas present one year. It was a glorious rendition, in pastel, of Pinocchio. It hangs on the wall behind her bed and would grace any room.

There was a teacher of the deaf assigned to the college,

without whose assistance Rebecah would not have made it through. The academic side would have been too much. As it was, she missed and misunderstood much of what was said in lessons. The authorities later tried to axe this teacher, and he asked me to write to the them, pointing out the value of his position. I did so in a very positive way, and hope it paid off. People not involved with the education of the deaf have no idea of the difficulties.

Another person who came to Rebecah's aid was a young Norwegian girl on the course. She had, at an earlier stage in her life, experienced deafness through illness and knew what it was like to struggle to understand. Added to this was her experience of learning in a foreign language. She explained to me how she fully understood where Rebecah was missing out on the finer points, especially when being given instructions, so whenever her lessons coincided with Rebecah's, she would be there, interpreting and re-explaining. She was a great asset to Rebecah. Thank you, Anita, for your time, effort and caring.

Many of the language issues facing the deaf can be likened to a person learning in a foreign language. They grapple with the finer implications of words because those words have not been imbibed naturally through repetition, but learnt artificially through explanations of them, or dictionary definitions, or through reading them, none of which are quite the same. Reading can come the closest, but the deaf don't hear the amount of repetition of words that we hear. Just as foreigners struggle with our illogical grammar and syntax, so do the deaf.

Let us take time out for a moment, I will return to the acquisition of language at an earlier age, because it provides more easily understood examples. Here is a sentence: 'Daddy is rather a long time in bringing those sweeties to us, so we have to be patient.' You are speaking to a young deaf child. How many of those words would be meaningful? Can you guess? If you have established the signs or lip patterns for 'Daddy' and 'sweeties', that would be about it. The remainder would be facial expressions and body language. Similarly, 'I may go to the shops soon' would be translatable as 'I shop', with a point to the clock to understand soon, if the child is old enough to understand time. The deaf are not going to care which order the words take as long as the meaning is conveyed. This is how it works. Some deaf people do become proficient at written language, and this number is growing, but most of the deaf still struggle to some degree or other.

The skill in finger spelling is also lacking because they don't hear the audible breakdown of words phonetically, and rely more on the visual recognition; but as this is not accompanied by an internalised sound, it is a little more difficult to remember. Besides, reading itself can be quite an ordeal for deaf people unless the language is very simple. Simple language is usually accompanied by more childlike concepts, which can be an insult to their intelligence. Again, this is gradually altering and there is a new, up-and-coming breed of deaf children with amazing accomplishments.

There is the added difficulty of lip-reading. This in itself is a topic in its own right. At best only about thirty per cent of lip-reading actually is that. The rest is contextual guesswork with a mixture of body language and other factors. These 'other factors' are numerous. How lip-readable is the person? What is their mouth shape like, and do they have a beard? Do they know which words to emphasise, which to speed up or slow down? Is the sun shining in the deaf person's eyes as they are facing the speaker? Are they indeed facing you, and not constantly turning their heads as lecturers do, for example? Very importantly, how familiar is the deaf person with the topic being described? If you want to know how difficult lip-reading is, turn the telly down and try it. Try it on the news where somebody is just sitting talking, and then try it during a film when the action is there to help you. Remember, also, you *already have language* and are familiar with the majority of the words you are trying to lip-read.

I remember attending signing classes taught by a deaf person. Actually, in truth they were not very well taught. (I met this man as an examiner of sign language years later, and his teaching skills had improved enormously.) I struggled to read the signer and he collared me socially and wouldn't let me off the hook. I grew so tired of asking him to repeat, I pretended I understood. He knew, of course, and I was caught out in the next sentence. I just wanted to opt out and be left alone. That is how the deaf feel when with hearing people who don't make the effort to communicate. There is nothing sentimental about any of this. Unless you sign fluently, communication with the deaf, hearing person to deaf person, is hard work and ongoing. It is not interesting for half an hour, then give up and revert to 'normal'; it is an ever present struggle.

When Rebecah was in Belize and again in Africa doing ecological studies for the environment, she would find herself alone at night-time, with insufficient lighting for lip-reading, and people would forget, understandably, to include her (and I've been guilty of this myself, many times). I am talking here about a three-month stint and a seven-month stint respectively. She stuck it out, but it was hard and she often felt lonely. Night-times became an endurance test.

In Africa, Rebecah met somebody who could sign during a certain period there, and this was tremendous for Rebecah; but she eventually stopped. To use Rebecah's words, 'She gave up on me.' Rebecah still liked her and appreciated her, though. Always positive! This experience in Africa came as a terrific blow to Rebecah, and it was from the inner loneliness felt at this time that she determined the course of her life, which was to be constantly around deaf people, where she felt comfortable.

I accompanied Rebecah, at her request, in an interview for an art college. The interviewer was trying to tell us that Rebecah would be well catered for on her course. She was sitting with the light angled behind her in front of a venetian blind, which sent strips of sunlight across her face. When talking she hardly moved her lips. Rebecah hadn't understood a word, and asked me what it was all about when we left the interview room. Needless to say, Rebecah didn't choose that college.

The college she *did* choose in Middlesborough awarded her with a merit, and I think it was well deserved. The next step was university.

Before leaving Rebecah's childhood, there are some more intimate moments in the form of letters to home spanning the period of time from Mary Hare, to letters from Africa I have decided to share. I have focused on the more humorous and empathetic moments, which will give a first-hand indication of her struggle with language and of the sort of person Rebecah is and how she has developed, without my interpretation.

Letters Home, and Funny Times

THE SPOKEN WORD CARRIES WITH IT MANY INNUENDOS according to how it is said: 'I love you!' 'Very funny.' Sarcasm, dry humour, jokes, puns, English idioms, in fact all the things a foreigner would find difficult then so would a deaf person, probably. Certainly with Rebecah, linguistic humour has taken a long time to acquire. (This can convey a sense of immaturity to a casual observer, but the inner life of a deaf person is anything but immature, because great patience and one-pointed focus is required.) It is a common habit in which many of us indulge; that of judging people by their level of articulacy.

When Stuart and I were in Malaysia, before the children were born, Stuart taught in an English medium school. The headmaster, who was Malay, was giving a speech, addressing the whole school. In the middle of the speech, he interjected with an English idiom which went like this: 'And last night in bed, my wife was pulling my legs...'

Once an idiom is slightly wrong, it sounds funny to our ears, but you wouldn't detect this unless you had been brought up to hear the flow of spoken English. In this case, one letter – an 's' – made all the difference. This is how it is with the deaf. Looking at Rebecah's old school letters, these are the passages which both amused and touched me. The first one is, 'It was raining a cat and a dog.' Funny, as long as we laugh with her, and not at her.

Here are some extracts from Rebecah's letters, mostly from Mary Hare, but then moving on up to her time in Africa. These have been dated where possible to show the gradations in improved English and, of course, maturity. Rebecah was born in 1977.

Dated 1989:

> I am counting how many weeks are left. Only 7½ weeks are left. Exciting isn't it?

> My heart went very fast. My mouth is smiling most of the time, in the night, and sometimes in the morning. Is that the same for you?
>
> I bet you are! [*sic*]

Dated 1990:

> Dear happy family!
>
> Hi, it's me Beck. Thanks for you rang me which I was enjoyed to talk to you. Am I going to Emma's house on 16th Nov? or Dec?
>
> Well, please will you bring a flash which I've got a camera and a film in it. Every time when I saw the girls wore funny clothes in their droms [*sic*]...

I must explain that talking on the phone means using the minicom, a device which allows deaf people to type to each other, and that 'droms' means dorms, short for dormitories. This practice of getting consonants in the wrong place is a common fault with Rebecah, a difficulty she still has, even now. I had always attributed it to her deafness and the ambiguities of lip-reading, but not all deaf children have this fault, especially after a three-year degree course. Stuart has recently suggested that it might be some form of mild dyslexia. I think he's right. Rebecah, however, adamantly refutes this.

Dated about 1990:

> There are two more people are birthday on this Saturday 21st at the same time. I've got their cards and no presents as well. DAWN IT (sorry about that for saying a rude word) [*sic*].

Dated 1991:

> On Tuesday morning, there was a man who was called Mr Warren. He comes from Australia. Do you remember that I told you that Miss Ogg exchanged Mr Warren from Australia for a year? If yes... Well he is nice person and he has quite lots of beard around his chin. He sang songs from Australia. I liked it and his voice was different from here...

I'm so happy because my cough is getting better. I think it is because of the horrible medicine that you brought me. But you mustn't buy me another if I get a cough. UNDERSTAND? I think it is so funny to say these words. Don't you think so?...

...Well ...Please can I have some more free letters from Daddy's work because I ran out...

I hope Daddy will have a good time in 'West Palm Beach' in Florida and he might get a tan from the sun. Lucky him. So am I but I won't get it from the sun easily.

I'm very sorry about those file papers. Please forgive me? I'll try to write you another lovely letter.

(Sorry about the small grammar!) [*sic*]...

Aged about thirteen:

...My friend Charlotte moved her house to Surrey [*sic*]. She has a swimming pool which belongs to her. She said that she didn't want it because it was by the water, so she will change the swimming pool into a fishpond!

SORRY I must go now. I'm telling you the truth, I just can't wait to see you! I'm so exciting! [*sic*]

Aged sixteen:

I also saved myself for not going to someone's houses just for the weekend because of the exams that are coming up fairly soon. I know it's possible for me but I can try because I like working in some ways! This weekend, I've 3 big sheets to do for my art project. A lot of work is needed to be done. Another working weekend! [*sic*]

The English, as you will observe, has by this time improved considerably.

Dated 2000, in Africa:

Lets change the subject, once the choo (loo) is completed, I bought a cheap pair of flip flop to save time in buckling up my sandles. I was rather plsed with them. I used my feet to shove the metal ring off the hole for my incoming wee! Once I did that, the

> edge of the whole caught my flip flop and fell in the smelly pit hole. Oh no, it was 7ft deep. Certainly couldn't reach it by hand! Found 2 sticks long enuff to touch my flip flop as it lightly rested on top of the 'sewage.' Two pinpointed sticks were hopeless together and it fell once again. This time it went in between a cut through the beauty sewage. I reported it to the camp leader about the stupidity of my incident. He came up with the idea of a hook-wire or wood. On our way to the choo, one frontier guy came out from the cupicle (sp?). Just hope he missed my flip flop. The camp leader caught my flip flop by a hook and we both discovered that it already had been spat on! Phew. The whole crew of the Frontier laughed! hee [*sic*].

Dated 2000, in Africa (again):

> At the matatus bus (pretty uncomfortable as my friends called it 'death trap,') it was v. squashed up + sweaty when packed with 16/17 people on 13/14 seaters!
>
> ...I do not allow her to do everything for me as I'll find it offendive (sp?) She had 3 kids,- Susan and her brothers. She speaks English fluently and so is her signs.
>
> ...compared to me at the visiter house, I always have lovliest food and I'm gaining weights! Jeez, LOOSE is my desire NOT GAIN!
>
> Because I'm a visiter, teachers do have 2 faces [*sic*]...

Of course, amongst this is some very well written English describing profound and fascinating experiences, as well as the expression of her cultural insights.

Returning once again to Rebecah's early years, there is an incident which always stands out in my mind, which I would like to include here, even though it is not a 'letter from school'. It is an incident which I remember with such poignancy. Rebecah was about three years old, and we were going somewhere exciting at three o'clock in the afternoon. Rebecah wanted to go 'now' and didn't understand why we couldn't. I thought long and hard for a solution, and then had a brainwave. I showed her the clock, and explained meticulously that when that little hand moved on to the three, we would go. It was one o'clock at the time. A few minutes later Rebecah came up to me with great excitement, indicating that it was time to go. Dragging my hand, she took me to the clock. Sure enough, the small hand was on the three. How's that for intelligence! She had removed the clock and found the way to wind on the hands and return it to the mantelpiece. I hugged her, then began a new round of explanation. I think she understood, but I was never quite sure.

Watching films before the advent of subtitles was always a challenge, and on one occasion, funny. By the time I'd explained what had gone, we'd missed what was coming. (Signing would have been much easier.) One film in particular comes to mind. It was a John Wayne special, with fairly sparse and simplistic dialogue. I indicated to Rebecah to wait before explaining. She waited quite a long time, whilst watching the actors talk. Meanwhile I was trying to put together a meaningful synopsis of what was being said. I couldn't, and the scene changed. I gave her one sentence to convey everything. She looked at me and repeated the sentence back to me about six times, the implication being that they'd spent five minutes or so saying the same sentence over and over! I was not telling her the truth, or so she thought. To me it was so funny. I laughed and laughed. She remained baffled. It was her first attempt at sarcasm, but she didn't know it.

However, this changed when subtitling became more widely available. My thanks again go to those pioneering spirits who fought for it. The first subtitled film we watched as a family was *Splash* with Tom Hanks. We all laughed – together! What a relief, and what a joy! My first attempt at successful signing all the way through a film at the cinema was *Sixth Sense*. She was even able to explain the twist at the end to some very bright hearing people!

True Grit

I RECEIVED A PHONE CALL IN THE MIDDLE OF A HOT SUMMER'S day. It was from Rebecah. Any verbal phone calls from Rebecah are taken on trust, from her point of view. She can't tell a word I'm saying, not even 'yes' or 'no', although she has learned to differentiate between a man's voice and a woman's. Any phone calls received this way – and there have been many – have to be listened to carefully, because you can't ask for clarification and you can't defer any request, so it's down tools and do what is asked if you possibly can. This was a phone call asking me to phone the school to tell them where she was, which in this case was at a pub near a set of crossroads, just outside Hungerford. I dutifully made the call and the explanation came later.

Rebecah had gone on a sponsored bike race for charity. She was winning too, and this meant a lot to her, being the competitive girl she is. Well, she had forgotten the strapping around her feet on the pedals and tried to put her foot down on the ground, to steady herself, when taking a corner too quickly. Her foot of course was trapped and down she went. She banged her head and grazed her hands and legs quite badly. Grit from the road got into the wounds (hence the heading of this chapter). In her haste to remain ahead, she'd taken a wrong turn. She asked a passer-by to make a phone call on her behalf, but he indicated that he was too busy. Not being able to remember the school's telephone number, she rang me.

The school minibus came to the rescue, equipped with first aid kit. Rebecah climbed in, complete with bike. When the bus reached a point that she recognised, against the advice of the staff, she insisted on riding the rest of the way back to school on her bike, bleeding hands and all, and with no chance whatsoever of winning.

This is an extract from her letter describing the situation.

> On that day, we've raised about £2,000! A lot of money. It was great fun and I enjoyed selling the tickets to them!
>
> The next day, it was a 24 miles ride – you know what happened to me! A silly girl for going the wrong route to Hungerford. My hands get better now but my bruses – not yet!
>
> I couldn't write my prep on that nite as it hurt every time I bent my fingers! Therefore I've had a double prep on Monday's night.

In her entire life, I've never known Rebecah to feel sorry for herself or play the victim. Never! She has been stubborn and unfeeling towards me at times, but that has been the extent of her faults and I consider myself very lucky and privileged to have been her mum. The same goes for my son. I truly count my blessings in this department. I could not have wished for two more lovely children on this planet and I am eternally grateful. I remember a member of staff at Rebecah's school telling me how beautiful Rebecah was, and he concluded his remarks with something unusual, 'Thank you for producing her.' I was so moved, in fact I was near to tears. James too has similar stories, and although I feel I shouldn't boast about him too, there are one or two touches I'd like to add, just to enhance my story. I am, however, well aware that I don't have the monopoly on this and many parents have a story to tell.

James has often had to be Rebecah's 'voice' in growing up, and is very comfortable and patient around the deaf. His life is all the richer for the experience. More latterly, he has helped her greatly with her university work and has demonstrated endless patience, especially with regard to her stubbornness, which is largely born out of a desire to be independent. My husband too deserves to be greatly thanked for his patience and commitment in helping her. How many parents would take a week off work to help their child through their GCSEs? Without Stuart's dogged determination and patient input, Rebecah would not have done so well.

When Rebecah was writing the final dissertation for her degree, the computer crashed and she lost much of her work. This was a double blow, as not only does spelling and grammar have to be corrected, but also Rebecah believed that it curtailed her chances of a 2:1 degree. She had set her heart on this, as she so wished to be equal with the hearing world, as she saw it. She was patient as ever and started again, Stuart assisting her all over again. She worked through the night, with the deadline in mind. Later, as Rebecah was showing me how to use a computer and I was annoyed at it crashing, she told me not to worry, that it happens, and that that was why, in her opinion, she didn't achieve a 2:1.

I recently asked James what he *really* thought of Rebecah, and he said that he loved her company and adored her. Rebecah feels the same about him. That's not to say that they didn't have their jealousies and occasional fights while growing up. These incidents provide valuable learning situations on how to deal with negative emotions; that is, to feel them, acknowledge them and let them go. We all have to learn this. There are no exceptions. We all must learn how to deal with these things as part of our contract here on earth. Only when we've transcended the lower vibrations can we sustain the higher ones, otherwise we fall prey to them and live our lives tossed around like boats on a stormy sea, without much control of our destinies.

Our thoughts are so important in our endeavour to create our chosen reality. Watching James grow up, I noticed that he was often ready to be forgiving, and that if people were talking negatively about someone, he wouldn't join in. How to learn from your children! I too have stopped talking and thinking negatively (most of the time) but it's taken me a long time to learn, much longer than James. And do you know what? He leads a charmed life. Both he and Rebecah reflect that inner positivity and optimism on the outside, and it makes a difference to them. I can see that so clearly. They both make a lot of people very happy and as a result, are very happy themselves, particularly James. Rebecah has more of a struggle, for obvious reasons, but, you know what... again? Rebecah says that, given the choice, she wouldn't be hearing. Such are the opportunities afforded her on account of her deafness, and the happiness she experiences through camaraderie with other deaf friends.

Another little aside would be valuable here. James has imbibed much of my ethos on life. We have had many a discussion and he has read quite a few books recommended by me. When he was playing a lot of competitive tennis, growing up, he would often lose and, at first, lose face by being near to tears. Together we both had to learn to walk through this. It was a good exercise on staying present, forgetting the last point, on knowing that the state of mind was often the determining factor, and that in the final outcome, not taking things personally was the best way to handle things (rather like Rudyard Kipling's poem 'If'). I must add here that James told me how he dealt with taking things personally, both on and off the court. If something was said that he didn't like, if it didn't affect him emotionally, he'd ignore it; if it did, he'd deal with it, so it could be interpreted as a gift in disguise. James also needed to learn to believe in himself and not let that self-doubt that we all feel creep in and take over. Like the rest of us, again, he had to deal with fear – the fear of losing – which meant feeling it and going ahead anyway. A great teacher, sport...

I don't in truth think he ever preferred losing to winning – who does? – but we both agreed that it was best to end on a positive thought towards the opponent and look him in the eye and mean it, at the end of a match, win or lose. I don't suppose either that I'd make the best candidate for coaching Wimbledon players. In fact, one of his coaches told him to hate his opponent, something with which I did not concur, but I'd make a good candidate for a teacher of life: 'how to keep your vibrations high'.

James now captains the joint London Universities Tennis Team, and not being under any real pressure, his actual technical skills, which are considerable, stand him in good stead, as well as his ability to both organise and lead fairly. Watching him on the tennis court is like viewing poetry in motion.

Whilst on the subject of James, the following event happened at his first year in medical school. He phoned me, complaining of a headache, fever, sickness, swollen lips and tongue, and giving a general cry of, 'Help me, Mum!' Immediately food poisoning came to mind. I asked him where he'd been eating and, of course, he said McDonalds. I had told him earlier that his vibrations were too high for that, as their whole ethos was not one of love, but money at all costs, so I guessed as much; he had eaten there. I simply asked for healing for him, and perhaps my training in Reiki helped, but possibly stronger than that was my empathy as a mum.

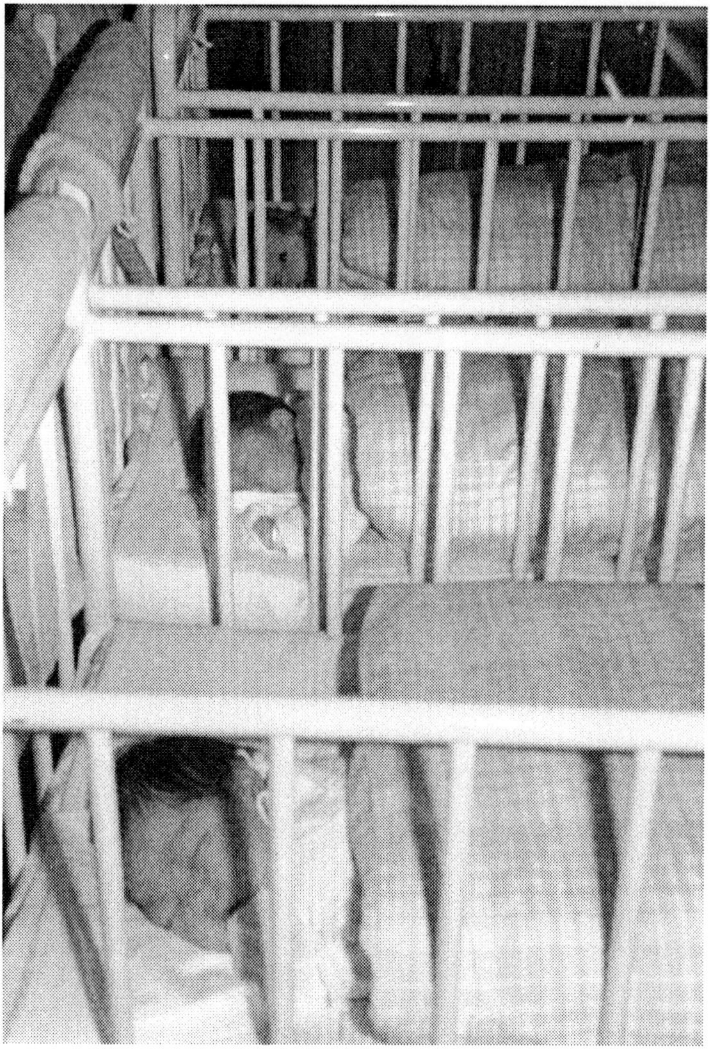

Rebecah (third back) at the Fatimah Hospital
in Ipoh, Malaysia 1977

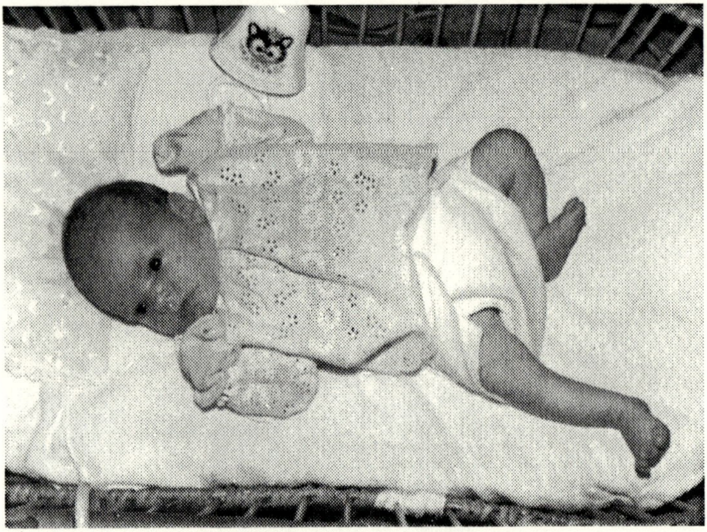

Rebecah at ten days old

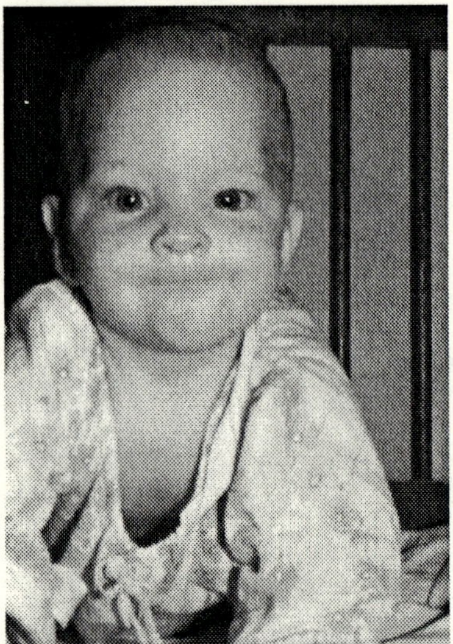

Rebecah just waking up

Rebecah in Cardiff

Rebecah, 3½, and James, 2

A Mothers' Day card made by
Rebecah at age 6 or 7

Rebecah at Boston Spa

Starting at Mary Hare, 1989

Rebecah as Head Girl in the Upper Sixth
at Mary Hare

Rebecah on holiday in Malaysia

Deaf girl wins through

Operation Raleigh hopeful Miss Rebecah Taylor overcame more obstacles than most to qualify for the adventure of a lifetime.

The 19-year-old went through the same selection procedure as everyone else, even though she is profoundly deaf.

Miss Taylor, whose parents live in Riverside Road, Richmond, attends a school for bright deaf youngsters at Newbury in Berkshire. Schoolfriends are helping her raise the £3,000 needed for an expedition.

She has chosen Belize in Central America as her destination. During the trip the group will work on four projects: research on management of forests, development of local health and education facilities, underwater surveys on the world's second largest barrier reef, and the development of a nature reserve, a joint venture with the Audubon Society.

Her mother, Mrs Jill Taylor, said: "She just wanted to do it. She read about it, and it is such a strong driving force with her to do it. She is a very out-door sort of girl anyway."

Selection involved a strenuous physical test with people she had not met before, including learning to trust others while blindfolded, which she found particularly difficult. She also had to give a talk to the group, and chose to speak about herself. She asked the group why they would not talk to her and then explained about her deafness and the ways she can communicate. By the end of the weekend she had overcome the communication gap and won many new friends.

Miss Taylor studies maths and art A levels at the Mary Hare School for the Deaf, where she is also head girl.

She wants to go on to an art foundation course before taking part in the Operation Raleigh trip in 1997. In the future, said her mother, she eventually wants to teach the deaf.

Referring to the trip, Mrs Taylor added: "It is a driving force to do something she loves and help others. Ever since she was a little girl, if I left her outside she could always occupy herself, she would do collages with nature. She was always fascinated with nature."

So far Miss Taylor has organised a 12-hour sponsored disco to raise money and has applied to various people for grants. Her major fundraising efforts are having to take second place to her studies and duties as head girl.

Adventures ahead for Miss Rebecah Taylor

Newspaper clipping from the Darlington and Stockton Times, Saturday February 17, 1996, about Rebecah's acceptance on Operation Raleigh

Rebecah with The Kerugoya School for the Deaf in Kenya, 2000

A recent photograph of Rebecah on holiday
in Barbados, 2000

James on holiday in Barbados, 2000

A series of photographs showing strange images that appeared after developing

Cousins Thomas, Kate, Abigail and Charles.
To the left of the tree is a gnome-like figure

Christmas time at home in Richmond. Two fairies appeared after developing, one to the left of the king and another in the bottom right-hand corner of the second windowpane up

Rebecah in Leeds, 1998. There's a strange figure in the bottom right of the tree

Kenyan National Park, 2000.
On the left is the man who was thrown by a cheetah

James rang the next day, saying that immediately on putting the phone down he felt better, and was completely recovered within two hours. Now these kinds of miracles are rare, and I'm not as yet aware whether they will or will not happen in any given situation; but they do, from time to time. I trust that this power to heal both ourselves and others can only become stronger as our awareness and love for ourselves and each other grows. Indeed, this was a good start to medical school, don't you think?

I am a teacher, and whilst at school the other day, a colleague asked me what sort of things Rebecah had done in order that I should write a book about her. Trying to describe such things from an outsider's perspective was quite a challenge. I often find myself challenged in this way; that is, having to find words to describe external actions or events, when the value of something, for me, is primarily in the inner understanding of what such events have to offer. There is not always very much to describe in the way of 'incidents'. More than this, the real value of life is in the state of being; this is not always provable and not always outwardly demonstrable. Sometimes an external event may be accompanied by an inner knowing as to why it happens, but my understanding and experience of such events and subsequent emotional reaction is unorthodox, so I don't have the usual comments.

An example of this can be seen with regard to the foot-and-mouth disease at the moment. To me, it is not as awful as people think, because our treatment of animals is barbaric anyway, and we need to see this and shift on in our consciousness. Would we treat children this way? Would we treat dogs this way? It is also my understanding that in making this sacrifice – i.e. being slaughtered en masse – those animals are helping our evolution by showing us that not only do we not need to eat meat (although I am aware that this is a choice), but that animals have souls and feelings, and are evolving like us, and we need to be caring towards them. As a result of their help, in showing us this, the animals will perhaps move on in their own evolution, and take on a higher form of life in their next incarnation, wherever and whatever this is.

It is also my understanding that the disease is spread on more of a conscious level than a physical one, and that vaccines won't prevent a thing. They rarely do, anyway. The disease itself, I understand, is really nothing more than a common cold and not a threat at all. At some level of our own consciousness we've created this situation for ourselves, because we won't learn. We rarely notice the outcomes of our own creation because we don't link things on a consciousness level and because there is usually a delay between our actions and the outcome, so we don't connect the two.

This is not orthodox thinking, but how do I convey any of this in a casual conversation? The animals have given of themselves in service. Do we revere them and thank them for making the sacrifice for us? Do we pray for their souls? The native American Indians did. If cows were to talk they might say, 'You see those humans over there? Well, they take us away in vans to slaughter and eat us.'

'No, impossible!'

'Yes, that's the only reason we're here, from their point of view.'

'Never! What utter nonsense. Carry on and eat the grass.'

And if the cows were even more intelligent they might say, 'This so-called disease of foot-and-mouth is only like a common cold; anyway, there's an alternative agenda here. Besides, humans have deliberately created disease – like the ones which have been unleashed in Africa – through their secret military operations and germ warfare. They treat their own people in this way. They consider them as... wait for it – *cattle!*'

And the people would say, 'Never!'

Similarly, if I'm trying to describe inner states of knowing or experience, this can become difficult, as what the words convey in terms of my own understanding do not necessarily convey the same understanding in others. Often an attempt to explain something of this nature, which has profound significance for me, undermines the quality of my own experience, so invariably I keep quiet. However, sometimes I am pleasantly surprised as somebody *does* understand and can add something, expanding my own perspective. Usually what happens is that I modify my words to a level that I think is acceptable to the other person, throwing in just a little of my own truth, and this too is wholly unsatisfactory. Don't we all do this to some degree or other?

So, on this occasion, I managed to find 'external events', which I hadn't thought of relaying, and yet another gift from the gods – in the form of this lovely lady – was bestowed upon me. I just need to trust more that nothing is without reason, but it's sometimes hard to believe that. The following, as a result of that conversation, is what I would like to share.

University

Rebecah's entry to university was not quite straightforward. She had completed an arts foundation course and was about to enter university or art college and embark upon the usual three-year degree course. I accompanied her to an interview at an art college in London, as London was where she wanted to be. She failed to gain entry and was, of course, very disappointed. I felt that this was a blessing in disguise, as there was something not right about the whole thing. She had already told me that her heart wasn't in art any more, so acceptance to art college could have been a nightmare and there would have been little in the way of deaf support.

We looked around various universities and eventually settled on Wolverhampton, where the deaf support was substantial, if not wholly adequate. However, she wished to change her degree from art to environmental science. Her A levels were in art and maths, so this could have been a major setback. One of her favourite subjects at school had been geography, which she had failed at GCSE level. She had cried buckets over that. (She gained only a grade D.) Her other five subjects were As and Bs, and I was so proud of her, in science subjects too – something which I never achieved. I told her not to say a word and trust that she would get where she needed to be. She entered university having applied as an art student. A little way into the course she asked to change to environmental science. She was accepted, which was wonderful, at first; the first hurdle jumped, as it were. What followed was not quite so easy.

Having changed subjects, she didn't have the background

knowledge. There began a year of focused attention, beginning as far back as GCSE level and moving on to 'A' level until she had grasped the subject well enough o tackle it at degree level. She also had to catch up on what she had missed at the beginning of the course, reading up on lectures that were not accompanied by a signer, and learning masses in the way of new vocabulary. Then there was the added problem of the English, which she finds difficult anyway, and she was certainly not used to writing in the scientific style expected of her. All her grammar had to be checked and essays rewritten before she could submit them. In all honesty, most people would have given up. Added to this was the complication of fieldwork, where lip-reading the lecturers and grasping instructions around groups of hearing people was almost impossible at times.

Lectures accompanied by visual input such as slides were only half understood, as she couldn't take her eyes off the signer. Rebecah would often find herself in a subservient position, having to ask students for their time in explaining things. Many of them were glad to help and admired her for her tenacity. Not all the signers were proficient at each subject at degree level, which created further understandable difficulties, and were often too busy to provide additional assistance. One lecturer was highly critical of the standard of her English, which knocked Rebecah off her pedestal, and my husband did actually interfere at this point, saying that that was like taking her to the top of a bridge and pushing her off, and that if he knew what it had taken for her to be where she was, he would have a rethink.

Here is Dr Ken Addison's own account of what ensued from that incident:

> Rebecah came to Wolverhampton at a time when Higher Education was not just proactive in expanding access to students with learning difficulties, who might have found an undergraduate career previously too daunting, but was also aware of the future extension of the Disability Discrimination Act to HE in the form of SENDA – the Special Education Needs & Discrimination Act (2001). The University of Wolverhampton was fortunate to possess an excellent Communications Support Unit (CSU), for students with hearing and sight impairment,

which also shared some prominence with the Lighthouse Centre in the television series *See, Hear.* These may well have been instrumental in Rebecah's university choice but, in common with HE in general, specialist support was harder to back-up with a rapidly expanding demand for trained signers and note-takers.

In my role as Special Needs Tutor (SNT) in the School of Applied Sciences, working at the interface between academic and laboratory staff with the students for whom learning support was intended, I was acutely aware of difficulties in matching students' needs with appropriate support in a complex timetable and at a time of high demand. Rebecah's path inevitably crossed mine soon after her transfer into the School, as both SNT but also as one her lecturers in the course of her studies. Like so much of her mother's story, my recollections of Rebecah's progress towards successful Honours graduation are anecdotal, commencing with the singularity of her father's visit to Wolverhampton.

Concerned that Rebecah's achievement of a university place and progress towards the pinnacle of her formal education should not be undermined by signing/note-taking support, he asked for a meeting. Parent/academic staff meetings are usually confined to brief encounters, when slighlty embarrassed students sporting their MP-3 players and, maybe, carrying the odd desk lamp are directing their grossly-overloaded pack-horse parents to or from campus, chance upon one of their tutors. It is rare, and often only *in extremis,* that any more formal meeting occurs. I was therefore somewhat apprehensive at meeting Rebecah's father but also almost instantly put at ease by his very reasonableness and a distinct wish to make it clear that he wasn't undermining his daughter's ability to act for herself – something I felt she was keen to avoid. Apart from seeing that Rebecah was settled into her new surrounds, his point about the learning support was simple but profound – *'give Rebecah the tools and she will finish the job.'* I realised how much of her progress to that point was summarised in his exhortation and it remains a telling stage in my development as a supporting academic.

At the start of her second year, Rebecah participated in a ten-day field course based at Penrith. Now, full risk assessments have to be completed before each and every element of a field programme – and a second version for students with learning needs which carried specific risks. Jill Taylor has alluded on the quite different setting and challenges that the outdoors provides for deaf students including the cacophony of student voices shouting instructions and measurements and the noise of wind and water in exposed places. One particular recollection of Rebecah during this time was, by contrast, a moment of tranquillity and tranquil beauty. Our group was crouched below the wind beside Braithwaite's Wife Hole, a deep solution hollow on the limestone pavement on the west flank of Ingleborough. Professor Trueman, the group's plant ecologist, was carefully expounding the structure and edaphic significance of one of the limestone grassland's diminutive specialist plants. Our other deaf student had wandered off, leaving the fieldwork task to her notetaker, and there was the usual small cluster of students – on the upwind periphery of the group and thus out of earshot – either trying to look focused or simply gossiping. Only one student – Rebecah – was unequivocally on task, sitting cross-legged before the eminent Professor, looking intently from plant to the words spilling off his lips and back to the plant again, not daring to miss a thing. Apart from my delight at observing this silent moment of learning, the reader may also imagine what I *might* wish to say by way of chiding those fully able students who make less of their talents than they might!

My final anecdote comes from January in Rebecah's final year when her student cohort came to the illustrated oral presentations of progress towards their Honours Projects, before a group of peers and tutors. This is another area in which SENDA requires our sensitivity to students with respect to means of assessment and the need to vary its form in appropriate cases – but there was never any doubt that Rebecah would insist on giving anything other than a conventional presentation. Thus her research, on boat-induced erosion to the shoreline of Lake Windermere, was delivered orally to a suitably-impressed audience and only with minimal support of a signer for the question and answer session. Six months from graduation, she had finally reached the level of achievement and maturity aspired to by all students and it was a privilege to sense it.

I have no way of knowing, and can only imagine inadequately, the internal fear, apprehension, perhaps panic or just plain uncertainty – and frustration, sense of loss or inadequacy and many, many more emotions besides – that students like Rebecah must feel about their disability, thousands of times during their lives. Rebecah showed lots of frustration, usually with herself

> over new ideas better explained when she had sought out the answers, but I never detected self pity or even a sense of unfairness or privilege towards her peers. Instead, as her mother's story tells, my recollections are of the intensity of her search to learn and determination to do well and minimise her disability; and of the specific intensity of her blue eyes as she sought to compensate for her deafness – and her almost never-failing, warm smile which told you that all was well again in her world! Not only was Rebecah a delight to teach and support in her learning but she must appreciate how much she taught us too – and how much this will improve, step by step, our ability to educate her successors.
>
> Dr Ken Addison, April 2004

Rebecah was, in short, a 'role model'. He achieved her degree! Wow! Enough said.

Operation Raleigh

Another incident demanding 'true grit' was during the selection process for Operation Raleigh. During a gruelling Outward Bound course, held on the moors, near Hebdon Bridge and in the pouring rain, all the participants were blindfolded during a team effort to ford a river. This meant that Rebecah was both deaf and blind. I felt at the time that this was just a bit too much! Few on the course, team leaders included, were deaf aware, anyway. The first night had been spent looking for food during the night, with little or no sleep. The second evening was spent indoors with each person giving a talk on a designated subject. Rebecah couldn't understand the vocabulary, so refused to give the talk, but they kept insisting. Eventually it was agreed that she talk about her deafness.

She told them many things and amongst them was the fact that she was well loved and that her parents took time with her, which was not always the case with some deaf children. She spoke too of the difficulties of acquiring language from being a young girl. By the time she had finished her talk (and I'd love to have been a fly on the wall) it seems people were overwhelmed and several came up to her, saying that it was a privilege to know her and that they hadn't realised the immensity of the problem. Out of forty people, ten were chosen. Rebecah was one of them.

Most of the selection process for Operation Raleigh involved motivated and stable young people, but it was not always the case. Rebecah developed a reputation for being able to handle the most difficult and destructive of people, and was sometimes assigned to work with them. She did so, admirably. The accolades awarded to her when the Raleigh session dispersed were fantastic. Rebecah, however, has forbidden me to include them here. I shall respect her wishes. Suffice to say, they rang her to ask if she would like to go for an interview to be on the staff, knowing that she was deaf. She was in the middle of her degree at the time so, unfortunately, couldn't take them up on their offer. I think, however, that she would love to do just that, at some point in the future.

Extraordinary Connections

THERE HAVE, AS THE TITLE OF THIS CHAPTER SUGGESTS, BEEN some remarkable and extraordinary connections with people, the like of which may have only been tenuously linked with Rebecah, but were, nonetheless, connected at some level. By far the most outstanding of these was an experience I had after the death of Princess Diana.

I was attending a spiritual workshop in a large house belonging to some friends of mine. Whilst there I began receiving a message, not in words, but just as an inner knowledge, to go and sit in the study, which was a fairly quiet place to be in a bustling household. As I sat quietly, the room began to fill with love. It was much more than the earthly kind of love and was quite overwhelming. What's more, it was the love of Princess Diana, along with her presence. It took me quite a while to believe this for myself, and I spent some time denying it – a 'this can't happen to me' scenario. But it was unmistakeable, as was the message. As I write this now I keep wanting to go downstairs and make cups of coffee because the experience was and is so sacred to me and precious, that I wish to delay and savour its telling. The feeling in my body is one of inner peace, love, excitement and connection to higher things. There is the eternal hum of the universe in my ears. My throat is somehow open and I become a channel, through which words can flow.

The first part of the message concerned my ability as a mother, which I took to be somewhat complementary, hence the connection with Rebecah. Diana wished me to somehow transfer my mothering abilities to William and Harry. I took this to mean 'surrogate' mother, and although I believe that anything is possible, this was just a bit too much at this stage in our evolution – for obvious reasons – so in this aspect of the interpretation I guess I was just feeling her thoughts, rather than being requested to follow instructions. I'm told that those on higher dimensions, looking down, see a more comprehensive picture of things (rather like looking down from a low-flying aeroplane), as well as seeing at more of a soul rather than purely physical level. The mother of Dominic, who I mentioned earlier, told me that she had had similar experiences, just before we met. Diana herself, in a channelled book called *Diana*, talks of having come to many of us after she left the earth plane.

I agreed, that day, to write to William and Harry; and certainly even now I have a strong desire to do so, but feel that I can't convey what I need to in a letter, and still await that 'special moment', that 'right opportunity' to write to them or even meet with them one day. This may or may not be and I'm not attached to the outcome one way or another. The desire to be of service is there and that has gone out to the universe, and along with it a trust that everything is as it's meant to be. What is interesting is that a friend told me that as far as he was concerned, we were definitely meeting up on the inner planes (the astral planes, the dream state world, whatever you wish to call it). I have dream memories myself of certain things, but can't be sure at this stage that they are any more than that, that is to say, if they have any 'reality' substance to them. Secretly, inwardly, I feel that they do, but I can't be certain.

Diana's presence felt as if it were in two parts. There was the earthly part, still a loving mum attached to her sons, as described above, and the evolved part, which understood the whole picture. There was no doubt about the second part of the message from her to me, and that was to write down everything I knew about her death and what surrounded it. She did not depart from my presence until I agreed to do this. I wrote to her brother along with many others, saying that I was grateful for his honesty in the speech at the funeral, and that it was a relief to hear it. I have written a poem, which is fairly comprehensive, and I am writing this now. The poem will be enclosed at the end of this chapter and is for the discerning reader.

Rebecah knows, very well, a young deaf actor, who played a silent role in the film *The Beach*. Rebecah said that he had a ten-minute signed dialogue in the film, but that it was cut. This young man has his own house and business in London and is doing very nicely, thank you. He asked her to go along with him to a dance where she could meet the film crew. Rebecah, however, declined, being loyal in honouring prior engagements. Ramon, her friend, admired her for it. Well, there are some unusual qualities in these young deaf people! I don't think I'd have turned down an opportunity to meet Leonardo DiCaprio at that age, do you? But for a young deaf person who hardly speaks to be commercially successful – in fact rich, by most people's standards – says a tremendous amount about how far we have come; and to demonstrate the point I shall relay one or two tales concerning deaf people, closer to my own generation and earlier, later in the book.

At a wedding reception held at Durham University, Rebecah and I found ourselves sitting opposite David Bellamy, the famous botanist, here in England. The circumstances leading up to our being there in the first place were unique and tell an interesting tale of how our lives are mapped out, rather like a computer game; many options to arrive at a certain place!

I was sitting in my home by myself, overlooking the river. At about the same time and unbeknown to myself, a young man was sitting opposite, on the far side of the river, wondering what it would be like to view the scenery from this house. As I sat and pondered, I thought I heard a scream coming from the area of the nearby waterfall, and had the thought that someone had severely hurt his or her back on the rocks. I stared out of the window, pretty intently, but put it down to my imagination and left to join my sister for lunch.

Something prompted me to leave my sister's house early, and as I arrived home and was putting the key in the door, a young man from behind me asked if he could use the phone to call an ambulance, as someone had fallen near the waterfall and hurt their back on the rocks! I thought this strange, as I don't usually get premonitions. It was the same young man who had been sitting opposite, but he didn't realise that this was the house he'd been longingly staring at. He'd tried one or two houses but had had no joy. We dutifully made the call and the ambulance arrived.

Alastair, the young man, went on with his tale, saying that there were many people, most of them tourists, and the people concerned could have asked anyone for help, but singled him out from quite a distance. He just happened to choose Richmond as a stopping-off place on a bike ride from Bishop Auckland. So we became friends. He met the family, and in fact Alistair and I have enjoyed many hours playing flute duets together.

At his wedding two years later, I sat and interpreted, verbally, between David Bellamy, the botanist, and Rebecah. He was wonderful with her, put his arm round her and said how much the world needed people like her and that it was especially good that she was deaf and doing such work. Rebecah is currently in the Philippines with 'Coral Cay Conservation', which is headed by – guess who – David Bellamy!

Rebecah was at home when Barry Brailsford stayed with us on his travels. What a privilege that was. Barry, better known in New Zealand than England, is an historian and archaeologist, and more latterly has had journeys that have taken him into the realms of sacred truths and ancient knowledge by invitation of ancient tribes such as the Aotearoa and the Hopi. The accounts of these tales are written in a number of books like *Song of the Stone* and *Chronicles of the Stone.*

During a talk he gave here in Richmond, Rebecah attended and was assisted by Vivien, who signed for her, but it was all a bit too abstract for Rebecah, and she left early. However, I did walk in on the two of them eating lunch together and conversing nicely. They made the connection they were supposed to make, and before leaving Barry gifted both Rebecah and myself with two of his stones each, one white and the other green. It was quite an overwhelming moment and I was stuck for words. He will return, as promised, and perhaps then or perhaps later Rebecah will understand her connection with him (and perhaps myself too). It will be exciting when she does, as they are both people of the earth. And in my book of life, nothing is a coincidence. Barry, I think, knew something of his link with Rebecah!

I picked up a magazine and found in it an article by Barry Brailsford. Here are three short excerpts from that article.

> Throughout the '90s, at the behest of the elders, I had carried greenstone to many nations. Others also took up that work, and it travelled far to sit within the seats of power, on the desks of presidents and prime ministers and in the hands of wisdom

> keepers and healers. Yet in all those journeys I never carried whitestone. However, my journey in the middle months of 2000 to the USA, Canada, England, Scotland, Finland, Estonia and Hawaii was quite different.
>
> ...Then he brought me to a startling moment of insight. George ended his account by explaining that the final part of the ceremony involved guests from afar, Maori elders from New Zealand, who gifted two large white stones to mark the new way of the path of reconciliation...
>
> ...Thus did two stories join to assure me that in carrying whitestone alongside greenstone, I was moving in accordance with something written long ago...
>
> ...It is a wondrous time of renewal for all, a truly remarkable time to be making a journey that brings us to deep wells of understanding.

As I write this I feel deeply connected to something, yet I know not what. This frustrates me. I am also reminded of a recent conversation I had with Rebecah. She told me that she felt guilty for not reading more spiritual books, but instead loved to go on these adventures with the earth. You can imagine my reaction to that. The earth is your spirituality. Your joy is your spirituality. There is no progress above without connection to the earth, our Mother. I wish I had Barry's and Rebecah's affinity with the earth. One day... soon!

At Mary Hare School, there was this rather cool 'dood' called Bernie Prior. He was the caretaker of the school, which was very appropriate, as he 'took care' of them all in more ways than one. Rebecah used to tell me that members of staff often commented on how calm he was about each problem, and how nothing fazed him. Well, Bernie used to meditate, amongst other things, and began to teach staff and pupils alike some techniques, and hold classes on self-awareness. It was on one of Bernie's weekend workshops held here in my home town of Richmond, that I had my experience with Diana.

I agreed to attend one of Bernie's spiritual weekend workshops, and then realised that it clashed with my parents' fiftieth wedding anniversary celebration. My priority was Bernie, so I gave my little dilemma to the universe. Having already read Bernie's literature and replied to it, it was a fait accompli as far as I was concerned. I called Bernie to say that I had filled in his form accepting a place on the course and had put it in the post. This, as far as he was concerned, was a miracle – because the literature for the weekend course was still being printed and certainly had not been sent out! I described the leaflet and the information on it and it was exactly the same as he was printing out at the time. When I later saw copies of these leaflets, they were exactly the same as the one I'd received. I remember Bernie's words: 'The gods have smiled on you.' This was some sort of miraculous time warp.

Bernie subsequently decided to make it a one-day workshop only, which meant that I was able to attend my parents' wedding anniversary celebrations after all. And so, my advent into 'miracledom' was beginning, or so I thought! It didn't continue!

Diana

Starlight from Sirius to earth she came
The Queen of our hearts, and her love did sustain
Through all her trials and her suffering
She made hearts dance and she made them sing.

Her life was open and others could see
Their pain was like hers, so how could that be?
With all the wealth and status bestowed
That was not enough; she needed strength to be bold.

To be a victim did not make her whole
So she forged her way through, created her role
Politically free, unrecognised Royalty –
There was less control
Allowing her to be free.

Full of grief herself, yet was able to give,
And give she did so that their hearts could live.
She gave to those children who were dying of cancer,
Made their grief her own, and that was part of her answer.

Class did not bar her, she saw the essence within
And her soul and her force field flowed through everything.
Her clothes and appearance gave the finest array
And her eyes shone behind them and did ever portray
The sadness she felt as she found her way.

So to Africa she took both love and hope
To walk in the minefields, from safety elope,
To walk amongst peoples of grief and despair
To try to enfold them, their lives to repair.

Her sense of fun – and that 'giggle' not right –
Ran like a thread of golden light
And soon she realised that emotion expressed
Could replace the bulimia, so sadly repressed.

So much was centred on William and Harry,
And now love with leadership they can know how to marry.
This has not been so for a very long time
But we've tasted it now, she's created a vine,
Which can take root and grow around the earth
And her timing was perfect for the time of new birth.

At the time of her death, two others died too.
There was Mother Theresa, how her aura grew,
There was MSI in North Carolina,
Few on the planet have attained to a finer
Degree of self-mastery, though to many unknown,
And each raised the vibrations to a specified tone.

And thus there was formed a trinity
Complying universally with the law of three
A new trinity is yet to emerge –
The mystery behind? Our inquisitive urge.

Diana showed us how one of high birth
Could be humble and gracious, yet well serve the earth,
Being human and normal we could identify
And the grief of her death was our own grief – why lie?

Into the arms of Christ she flew,
Brief return to her body, but knew she was due.
In the seventh dimension, being etherically prepared,
Now oversees life here with her love freely shared.

Theresa gave service of selfless devotion,
And showed how such fervour heals body and emotion,
Yet even in this there was limitation
Some rigid belief within such dedication.

MSI did much to raise the planet,
To raise consciousness and break people's habit.
And so with all three how could we fail –
To use their energy; help lift the veil?

When Diana died it created a portal
Waves of shock penetrated: Diana's immortal!
When shock such as this enters on a mass scale
It allows something in, something which could prevail.

It passed through our bodies and into the earth
And on and outward to the universe.
It bound us in honesty, allowed us to grieve
It was love, 'twas uniting; God's next plan to conceive.

As the funeral procession was underway
And extensions were made, allowing more sway,
The ley lines of London were rejuvenated
With love's energy, now transmutated.

The people's support and shared compassion
Like the loaves and the fishes, they knew no ration.
An electric stillness in the atmosphere
Erupted on hearing her brother, what cheer
And clapping, euphoric penetration
Into the Cathedral with such elation.

This fulfilled a mission of a cyclic course
As Christ lay vibrations linked with those and the Source;
An even cross marked her astrological date
Marking the new Christ era and sealing her fate.

She played her role fully, the legend Princess,
She knows that now she's had time to assess.
Her soul's great purpose, perfection in all
Her love and her guidance responds to our call.

Of Royal descent, of lineage connected
To Merovingian Kings, the bloodline perfected
And back yet further, and eventually landing
With Christ? The perfection beyond understanding.

Dodi and Diana were each a soul mate,
Not to be on earth but in heaven's state.
Diana the huntress, Dido the Greek,
Peace and some solace they could learn how to seek
Together in the tunnel of sacrifice;
They played their role and paid the price.

To serve humanity was their plight,
Yet to see the whole they've shed such light
There's no coincidence in God's creation
It starts from the core, then full radiation.

Queen of our hearts with truth in high estate,
Queen of diamonds, were their cries too late?
Or would they penetrate
In the aftermath, our souls?
Bringing honesty home from their sacrificial roles.

We can continue the work that she started
By sharing love, being open-hearted
And radiate from our own core
God's light and love, His perfect law;
Her life will then not have been in vain
We are just like her, in fact we're the same;
Let's prepare to change our lives' full range
Of work and home and education –
Our choice to do such wonders comes through
The world is ours, it is our Creation.

Diana *Explained*

THE OPENING LINE REFERS TO THE PLANET, WHICH DIANA'S soul may have visited at some time – as, I believe, both Rebecah and I have. It is my understanding that we are seeded from different planets and that we reincarnate many times, but that the soul essence, which is who we are, remains the same. I have vague and fleeting memories of being on Sirius myself with Rebecah, as I mentioned earlier, whom I saw as a dolphin at the time, strange as this may seem. I also feel that Diana and myself are from the same soul group, whatever that means, along with many others, of course, so it seems logical that we have traversed the same planes, so to speak. However this is only a guess on my part.

Diana came to me after her death and asked me to write to both William and Harry. I didn't, because I didn't know how to go about it. However, two subsequent promptings from her have persuaded me that I must, and what's more, I promised that I would. The reason I honestly felt that Diana approached me with this request was because I had been a good mother myself, and energetically, she would have picked this up. As anyone can imagine, her boys were of enormous concern to her.

Throughout much personal suffering, she was able still to help others. Many people would not be willing to do this, but the things we learnt about her after her death were extraordinary. She went to great lengths to help people and was consistent in her support of those people. They were often parents of children who had died, and her ability to feel for those people in their loss, reflected not only her deep love for her own children, but her own inner pain at never having felt really loved. Nobody else in the royal family has behaved in such a caring and personalised manner, and her behaviour highlighted this obvious discrepancy. We can only give to others when we know what it is to feel deeply ourselves.

Diana's life was made fairly public, and her various traumas, emotional difficulties, divorce, and the feeling of being alone, were shared by many people. In fact, there was hardly an aspect of her life which didn't relate to all of our lives, in some way or other, and people connected with her through this. They felt that they could, if they'd had the chance, have been her friend. Although I haven't made direct reference to this in the poem, she didn't do well academically, and yet everyone loved her. This proves that love is more important than academia, and yet people attach so much importance to 'cleverness'. Similarly, with Rebecah, she would not set the world alight academically, but her impact on those around her is considerable, and on a very small scale, like that of Diana's. And for her too, wealth and status weren't enough to make her happy either. Aren't these lessons we all need to learn? Wealth, status, privilege – none of those things were enough. She didn't feel loved either, so where could she turn?

The third verse refers to the word 'victim'. I remember reading an article about her that detailed an account of somebody advising her *not to be a victim*, in other words, not to blame others or to expect them to change, but to take life in hand and do it for herself. My goodness, how she did this! Similarly, so has Rebecah.

How she grew as a person was once again quite remarkable. Nobody told her to go and visit the homes of the suffering, and ultimately, the places where the minefields lay. She created that role for herself. It wasn't set up for her under royal protocol. Indeed, she didn't have the constraints of royalty, at that stage, or those of a politician. This allowed her a certain freedom to create her own role, and not all those in authority liked it. It exposed the politicians for valuing economics above the earth and life itself, and amongst other things, probably contributed to her 'end'.

In verse four I have said that giving was part of her answer, and it was, as she derived some comfort and satisfaction from this, but like many in her situation she still yearned for that single relationship that would fulfil her. We all want this, but it is really a deep yearning to feel connected to the Source of all that is – the Christ, or however you would like to word it. The other part of her 'answer' evades us all, I think.

So to verse five. Diana put people at their ease. A friend of mine met her in public. Ignoring all protocol, she headed straight for Diana and talked, saying that their lives were paralleled in so many ways. Much to the annoyance of the aspirational onlookers, their conversation lasted some time! Diana's response was that it was lovely to talk to a human being. She was able to relate to the soul of a person because she had so much soul herself. Diana was linked to the Source and knew something of her mission, though not the whole plan. That energetic connection which she had shone through everything that she did, even in her sadness.

Walking in the minefields was not only a journey of compassion, but it was a sign that she was willing to face her fears, even at the cost of her life. It was almost a prophetic gesture; a surrender of her life to the things that mattered most.

In verse seven, that '"giggle" not right' did indeed run like a thread of golden light. You see, the fact that Diana giggled a lot and sometimes at the 'wrong' times, was so funny and normal and endearing. It connected her to people in a way that was as precious as a gold thread, linking us all to her and each other through a common bond of humanity. It was her priceless gift, worth its weight in gold.

Bulimia often stems from a lack of self-worth. It could have even stemmed from some sort of unseen mind control, culminating in a lack of self-worth. Once Diana realised that she was able to tell certain people what was happening in her life, and more importantly, how she was feeling, she no longer needed to suppress her real self. Accepting who she was, meant that there was no need to harm herself, or indeed, be a victim.

The world has always wanted leadership it can love and trust, and so often we have been let down. Diana's love for the people was admirably demonstrated, as too was her love for her children, along with her openness towards them. Hugs were the norm and this was not in accordance with royal protocol; nor was it in accordance with many of the older generations within the Western world, and this too, hopefully, would make them sit up and think. What a fantastic thought; future leaders who could add kindness, love and compassion to their list! Three such leaders immediately come to mind. They are Gandhi, Mandela and the Dalai Lama.

Two other people died in the same week as Diana: Mother Theresa and somebody less well known, MSI, who reached quite a high level of consciousness, and who brought together many people. These people, through the work they were doing on themselves, helped lift the frequencies of the planet. The spiritual name for MSI was Maha Shivaratri, and he was a former pupil of Maharishi Mahesh Yogi. The people around Mother Theresa, and those who admired her work, would also help lift the frequencies, and similarly with Princess Diana.

When someone dies, energy is released on to the planet. When people of high calibre die, a high energy is released. Add to this the love from people who knew them, and the energy is enormous. Each of these people resonated to a different frequency; all love, of course, but with a slightly different emphasis. The emphasis from the MSI group was a conscious attempt at breaking habit patterns with a view to becoming enlightened. The emphasis with Mother Theresa was one approaching sainthood, where much needed healing was carried out, although there was some religious restriction here, and Diana had a worldwide appeal on many levels.

The combination of the frequencies emitted and the timeliness of their deaths, with regard to the planetary alignments, had a profound effect upon the planet, and probably ongoing from that, out towards the universe as we know it. My guess is that Diana had the greatest impact, as her fame was worldwide. The fact that there were three deaths is somehow significant with the universal law of three, as represented in Christianity by the Trinity. In early music three time was considered whole, and was represented by the circle.

Moving on now to verse fifteen, and continuing the theme of the impact of Diana's death, the first thing to notice was the shock this news created for humanity. When extreme shock hits us it can momentarily separate our other bodies from the physical, which in everyday life can serve as an awakener, to propel us on to a more profound understanding or realisation of things. It can also serve in allowing us to let go of something that we're unconsciously hanging on to. Here, in Diana's case, people grieved, on a mass scale, and unashamedly. Although their focus was Diana, what they often didn't realise is that they were grieving for the pain and suffering within their own lives. We are not taught or encouraged to do this, particularly in the West, and so much pent-up grief, anger, and resentment leads often to more stress and dis-ease.

On a more profound level, I believe that light entered the earth through our bodies, particularly around London where the funeral was held. You see, for that brief time, people were united, open and sharing with one another. The city gent would forget all barriers and stand willingly with a tramp; the so-called class system was, temporarily, not functioning. People shared food, so that there was abundance rather than fear of lack, which is what may have been represented with the 'miracle of the loaves and the fishes'. If that alone was all that was created by way of experience, then much would have been achieved, but there was so much more.

The funeral procession route required extension to accommodate the amount of people in attendance and I suspect, though I don't know this with certainty, that these extensions corresponded in some way with the ley lines of London. Ley lines are energy lines which the earth needs for her survival, rather like our veins and arteries. They connect churches and other sacred sites and are followed intuitively above the earth, in the form of a grid system, by migrating birds. London is a key and central point of focus on this earth, and once again it is my guess that it is the New Jerusalem that Blake talks about, and was somehow connected with the positive energy input at that time of Diana's funeral.

A number of factors have combined to give me this insight and some are a little difficult to put into words. My intuition told me that, as this cycle comes to an end, Diana's death and the beginning of this age, as symbolised by the coming of the Christ, were somehow linked. Diana was not a saint or an avatar, in the way that is Christ presented; indeed, she was very human, which was part of her appeal. But it is not on this level that the link is made.

Many people feel that they could never aspire to the level of Christ, and as such resort to revering or worshipping Him. I have always pondered over the words, 'What I do, all men can do.' And yet, we all know that we can't. So, what was the truth of these words?

With all the negativity of wars and thought patterns of hatred that this planet has had to endure, she (the planet) has needed a boost in order to stop her plummeting yet further into the depths, so that her evolution and 'ascension' can take place. The event of Diana's death has been a major contributory factor in this process, with the outpouring of love and transformation of people's personal grief, even though the outward focus was Diana. This grieving process was universally healing, though this may have been unperceived by many.

As the planet raises her consciousness, and to my way of thinking, earth is a sentient being, it allows those whose choice it is to raise theirs, to do just that. It is also my perception, and the perception of many, that this planet is ascending, or to put it another way, shifting to a higher octave. Although things may appear to remain stationary, in actual fact they do not, and life evolves or devolves. I suspect that the reason we don't easily observe this is because the timescales in which these things happen are so out of sync with our earthly lives. It is possible that the changes coming will be so great they are beyond understanding. Negativity is playing out now on a huge scale, but there are many who are working ardently for the light. Where do you, the reader, stand? It is a choice.

Legend has it that Christ settled in France, and that His children of Christ and their descendants became leaders, probably kings and queens, connected in bloodline to our kings and queens, and so Diana was completing a genetic cycle, as well as a 2,000-year 'energetic' cycle. Whether or not this is a literal truth, I have my doubts, but I do believe there is an unconscious – or perhaps subconscious – connection between the Christ figure and Diana, and that what goes on in the subconscious is often more powerful than what goes on in the conscious mind.

I don't know much about astrology, but apparently, her dates – wedding, death and so on – produced the sign of an 'even' cross, (as opposed to the uneven cross associated with Christ's suffering), the sign which the Hopi Indians said would herald in the 'new era'. Only twice in my life have I heard voices, and both times they came from the Hopi Indians, as clearly as if I were talking to you!

In verse twelve, I took this information directly from a channelled book, called simply *Diana,* and written by a Norwegian lady. In it Diana describes her life and perspective from the other side of the veil. On the impact of the crash, she had said that she flew onto the arms of Christ, but had briefly returned to her body, and felt the pain. She also said that she had been etherically prepared for the seventh dimension, whatever that means. (I have heard from other sources that she was lost for a time, immediately after death, because of the shock and suddenness of it all, and that as a result, she is very interested in rescue circles and other such groups who work with lost souls, or people who don't know they've died.)

Returning once again to the poem, and moving to verse ten, when Charles Spencer (who I acknowledge was no saint) made his speech, there was such euphoria because it was written with honesty, from the heart. I wrote to him at the time, thanking him. It was a huge relief to me, hearing it, because up until that point I had heard little that was meaningful, and I had been so affected by her death.

I wanted to scream from the rooftops. Other people recognised the truth of his words too, because the clapping started from outside the Cathedral where the service was being broadcast and moved into the Cathedral like a huge wave crescendoing into the hearts of us all.

There is another Christ-like connection I would like to share and it was also part of my personal experience. The day that Diana was killed was also the day when my husband and I had our wedding anniversary, and we were travelling to London to celebrate. On the journey there, on the motorway itself, the skies went black and the rains came down in torrents, making driving impossible, and the whole of the motorway traffic, where we were, came to a halt! It was eerie and ominous and immediately brought to mind the story of darkness, thunder and lightning descending after Christ's death. When a phenomenon so drastically hits many people on an emotional level, the impact on the weather patterns can be immediate and of the paranormal. I am told that such phenomena can happen in wartime when there is much focused activity on a certain outcome.

The references to Dodi and Diana being Greek refer to a Greek (or Egyptian) tragedy that they appeared to be enacting, that of Isis and Osiris, or Dido and Aeneas (a tragic story from the *Aeniad*). Their names were not dissimilar, and their lives did rather appear to carry a fatal attraction.

Mentioned in the penultimate verse are parallels between the life of Marilyn Monroe and Diana. Both were born on the first day of the month and married on the 29th of the month to men twelve years their senior. Both died at age thirty-six in the month of August. Do you remember some footage of Diana with William and Harry on a water slide? Diana was laughing and in that moment, carefree. Do you remember seeing some footage of Marilyn Monroe in a similar state of momentary joy? Was there not a resemblance in those moments? Didn't Elton John compose the one song for both?

There is much, much more I could say. This is only the tip of the iceberg. I was conveying something of this story in a spiritual meeting, not long after Diana died. Above my head and unbeknown to myself, appeared a golden cross (I hope it was the balanced cross) in confirmation of the truth, perhaps. I did, however, go on to say that Diana was of course murdered, and that out of this planned adversity came 'enlightenment', i.e. that which makes us lighter.

If the reader thinks that I am merely pulling together coincidences with regard to Marilyn Monroe, then consider the following extract. It was taken from a book, now out of print, by Lobsang Rampa, who, as mentioned earlier, influenced my life and the upbringing of my children.

> 1. President Lincoln was elected to Office in the year 1860. That, of course, can be ascertained from history books. So – Lincoln became President in 1860, and here is the first coincidence: Kennedy became President in 1960, a hundred years later.
>
> 2. President Lincoln was assassinated on a Friday. President Kennedy was assassinated on a Friday.

3. President Lincoln was at a theatre enjoying a stage show in the presence of his wife and he was then assassinated in the presence of his wife. President Kennedy was visiting Dallas, Texas, and he was riding in a car with his wife. He was also enjoying the show, that is, the show of public acclaim, etc.

4. President Lincoln was shot in the back whilst sitting in a box at the theatre. President Kennedy was shot in the back while sitting in a car.

5. President Lincoln was succeeded by a man named Johnson. Johnson became President after President Lincoln, but in Texas President Kennedy was killed and Vice-President Johnson was sworn in as President of the USA on board an aircraft bringing the body of the late President and the living new President back to the capital.

6. The Johnson who succeeded President Lincoln was a Democrat from southern USA; and Lyndon Johnson who succeeded President Kennedy also is a Democrat from the South – from Texas. So that is quite a set of 'coincidences', isn't it: though to show that there is more than chance taking part in things, enough to show that there must be some 'Divine Plan' making the entity that was president Lincoln perhaps come back as Kennedy so that a task could be accomplished.

7. Both the Johnsons had been members of the Senate before becoming President.

8. Lincoln's successor was Andrew Johnson. Now really read this... Andrew Johnson was born in 1808, but the Johnson who succeeded President Kennedy was born in 1908.

9. Lincoln was assassinated by a rather strange sort of a person, a thoroughly dissatisfied sort of a person if we are to believe the report, which is now history, and that assassin of Lincoln was John Wilkes Booth and he was born in 1839. Lee Harvey Oswald who, it was stated, murdered President Kennedy appears also to have been a very dissatisfied sort of a person, one who had been in trouble all too frequently. He was born in 1939.

10. Booth was assassinated before he could be brought to trial, but so was Oswald; Oswald was shot while being moved by the police, and before he could be brought to trial.

11. These coincidences, as you have seen, extend not only to the Presidents and their assassins, but also to the wives of the presidents because Mrs Lincoln, the wife of President Lincoln, lost a child while in the White House, and Mrs Kennedy, the wife of President Kennedy, lost a child while in the White House.

12. Lincoln had a secretary and that secretary was called Kennedy. Secretary Kennedy advised President Lincoln most strongly not to go to the theatre where he was assassinated. President Kennedy had a secretary also and he was called Lincoln, and secretary Lincoln strongly advised President Kennedy not to go to Dallas.

13. John Wilkes Booth shot President Lincoln in the back while the president was watching a show and then the assassin, Booth ran to hide in a store. But Lee Harvey Oswald shot Kennedy from a store and ran to hide in a theatre.

14. LINCOLN is seven letters, and if you count up KENNEDY you will find that it also has seven letters.

15. If you count John Wilkes Booth you will find that there are fifteen letters, and if you count Lee Harvey Oswald you will find that that has fifteen letters.

16. None of this has been proved, in both cases.

17. Ruby killed Oswald, Corbett killed Booth.

Lobsang Rampa goes on to say this. 'Now, do you seriously believe that these could be just coincidences? It isn't really possible, you know.'

I wonder, could Kennedy and Lincoln be the same person reincarnated? Could this somehow be a re-enactment of the same thing – with time, as we know it, not actually existing? This is too difficult to get our heads around, but we could at the very least chose to be open minded about it and not dismiss it.

My Story

REBECAH AND I CHOSE EACH OTHER, OF THAT I AM SURE IN my bones. That includes all the other members of the family too. We all chose each other. We pre-elected to give each other the experiences we needed in this life and it was arranged on the other side of the veil, so to speak, before we were born. We then forget everything and play out our lives in a way that maximises the experiences we need for our own growth. Towards the end of the book I would like Rebecah to say a little about her university years, her time in Africa, and, if she's willing, I'd like her to offer a few comments of her own. Just now, it is exciting for me to share with you some of the distinctive and deeply memorable experiences, which may shed some light on why Rebecah and I chose such a partnership.

My earliest and most profound memory was thinking that I wasn't going to die. I never knew what that meant and still don't – how can I? – but I am beginning to awaken to something within me that is so immense and so powerful that I feel like the 'incredible hulk' waiting to burst open. What I *do* remember is knowing instinctively that I couldn't share this thought with people. I didn't know why. It's taken me a long time to realise why we don't share our innermost thoughts, especially when they defy all logic or convention.

When you share something which you yourself hold to be a truth and somebody dismisses it, the energy of that thought becomes weakened and dissipated. What happens externally is that it doesn't hold he same importance to the person with whom you are sharing it, and that person can easily make a dismissive comment. This casts doubt on that belief and leaves you disappointed and with less hope, and with the wish that you hadn't shared it in the first place. (Alternatively, you may feel instinctively that the person will not understand, so you are wasting your time.) I'm sure we've all experienced this to some degree or other. Internally, these experiences close us down. Yet paradoxically, they serve us because if our personality can withstand such ridicule and abuse, our inner resolve can actually become strengthened. This 'inner resolve' has to become really rock solid, and it is this solid, unshakability that can make our dreams come true.

Thinking about Rebecah, I'd hoped for a miracle cure. When expressing this to someone, her response was, 'Well, miracles can happen, I suppose.' It was said in a very offhand way and left me feeling deflated. But I'm glad I was able to let go of the idea as quickly as I did, because it brought so many other riches into my life; the ability to let go and allow things to 'be' was one of them. And who knows, there might be a miracle cure, or not; it doesn't matter. Rebecah is a miracle in herself, anyway.

As a child I desperately wanted to see fairies, see ghosts; generally experience something of the fairy tale come true, but alas, nothing. This was the only memory that I brought with me, consciously, from my pre-existence – or, if you like, that higher part of myself, my soul. I was not gifted in the sixth sense department, so to hold steadfast to such a seemingly strange idea was something of an anomaly.

This underlying belief became part of a relentless driving force which has led me to many rich and varied adventures; some wildly unconventional. It has been a search for the truth, regardless of what others think. The realisation of the 'truth' in terms of actual experience has been for me a gradual process, with lots of little revelations along the way, but I am still 'veiled', so to speak. We all are, to one degree or another. However, the time is fast approaching when that will not be the case and all will be revealed. How do I 'know' this? I don't. Whatever I write here I cannot prove this to anyone, nor do I need to try, but a certain understanding has, if you like, been given to me, perhaps by the grace of God. A dear Catholic friend gave me this passage from the Bible – 1 Corinthians: 38: 'For now we see through a glass, darkly; but then face to face: now I know in part; but then shall I know even as I also am known.' I am assuming that most people on the planet will share a similar revelation.

Part of my journey has been about pushing back boundaries.

There is a paradox here. How can I push back boundaries if I accept what is? The clue lies in the attitude of mind. If I do what is right in my heart and am true to what feels right within myself, it doesn't matter how the outside looks, or about the outcome, so I can allow for many potential outcomes because I am not attached to them. I am content because I've connected with that something deep within that is real, and it is beyond emotion. In this way I feel, like many people, that I have grown, rather than remained static. I do admit, though, to having many moments when anxiety and self-doubt creep in. At one time, I pushed back my own boundaries too severely, rather than gradually, without being clear about my own feelings, and it resulted in my falling flat on my face, metaphorically speaking.

Being clear about one's own inner truth can often mean working through layer after layer of fear-based emotion before accessing it. This can be a difficult and painful process, but one worth pursuing because hanging on to the fear is actually more painful than facing it and letting it go. It is easier than constantly appeasing another, to keep the peace, while living a lie, and so making us angry on a deeper level. We all know that one, don't we? The process is often best highlighted for us in partnerships, with parents and other family members. This is why we chose them. They serve us in letting go of our fears and coming closer to who we really are. They are a gift in disguise, are they not?

I am a flautist. It has never worried me that Rebecah could not here music, or the birds singing, or any of those things more finely tuned to the frequency of hearing. It has concerned me that she could not always understand the finer points of language. What I am beginning to realise is that Rebecah 'hears' exactly what she needs to hear and understands what she needs to understand. She has, however, travelled solo round Africa. I wonder what she didn't 'hear' about that? Her journey is different from mine and because I don't know quite what it entails, I wouldn't dream of standing in her way in case it stopped her from seeing or knowing what she needs to know, or teach me, perhaps.

In pushing back my own boundaries, and subsequently the boundaries of others, it's been wonderful to watch the rigid belief systems of people erode in favour of much wider visions. People get stuck, and the older people become the 'stucker' they get, till they are so rigid and stuck they develop arthritis and other debilitating ailments. (This is obviously not true of everyone.)

How many people do you know who you can't converse with because they will disagree with just about everything you say? They haven't altered their belief systems in years, and there's practically nothing left to talk about. They can't even agree to differ, which is an essential ingredient in life. Just imagine what life would be like if they would open up a little. Take that a step further, and imagine how your own life would be enhanced if we allowed for the possibilities of more things being true. You could explore so many possibilities and life would become much more interesting, exciting, expanded and open, because you haven't closed it down. When I close down, my body feels it and I have less energy, but when I open, my body and mind become enthused with something and I feel more alive.

So, in breaking boundaries my life is often enthused with riches, and I never know from where they will come. I'd like to give an example. I have played and been involved with classical music since I was aged thirteen. About four years ago I went to a pub where they played tuneful pop and folk music, with a little rhythm and blues thrown in. I loved it and admired the musical expertise of the musicians, particularly the improvisatory skills, which I don't have.

Tony, who quietly and gently leads the show, asked me to bring along my flute. He always encourages people. I did so, but with great reservations, not, of course, having the music in front of me. He just kept encouraging me and told me to 'love my mistakes'. He's a devout Christian, not entirely of my own persuasion, yet the love, leadership, honesty, humour, tolerance, compassion and pearls of wisdom from this man are abounding. He walks his talk all right.

When we play together there is a magical synthesis of sound which takes me and others into other realms! I even had one couple say that they'd heard about my playing in Australia and they videoed me. When I play, people sometimes stop chatting and listen, because they want to; because I'm stopping them in their tracks and the more the people connect with me the better I play. I actually get a bigger high from it than I would in a concert hall. Something comes in to me. Perhaps I'm overshadowed by my soul in a way that doesn't ordinarily happen.

One week I got up to dance to the music, even though I felt ill. The music, coming from Mike, another regular artist, seemed to hit my body in a unique way. I could literally feel it in every cell, and my illness left me, quite miraculously. Everyone commented on how well I suddenly looked. Many times I feel 'transported', but not long ago I felt almost invisible, and certainly I felt invincible. There was not a trace of underlying anxiety in my body or mind. I was lifted onto another frequency and nothing could take me from that place of bliss for quite some time. Maggie, my friend, said that I seemed to disappear; an interesting choice of words because it wouldn't have surprised me if I had. In all my hours of meditation I've never been in that particular space.

Yet another experience was added to my collection only last week when we were treated to a drummer, who needed a hall twenty times the size. It was so loud we decided to commiserate by moving as far away as possible and generally behaving like young giggly girls. Once again I got up to dance and decided to move in decisive rhythms to the pounding of the drum. I also decided that rather than resisting it I'd choose to enjoy it; and I actually did so and got another of those 'highs', though not as strongly as the previous one, mentioned above. I wouldn't like to put this new 'skill' of mine to the test every week, however.

There is something in dancing; I think it has to do with the particle spin within the cells of our bodies that is, at least therapeutic, and at best partially enlightening. Many dance forms of different cultures spring to mind as I write this.

When Rebecah was in the final throes of university, she had to write an essay on dance, and had little in the way of time or resources in which to write it. She was at home and I didn't hold out much hope with regard to finding the right material in the local library and, in the dance section, I was right. I had a brainwave. Having scanned a few travel books in my time, I knew that they were often written with a great deal of fervour and passion, and a genuine 'feel' for the culture of the country being described. I found such a book on our agreed topic; Spanish dance.

On describing a local, non-touristic performance of the flamenco, there was a point in which it was said the performer would be willing to die within the dance, such was the depth of abandonment to everything but the active and all encompassing participation of the art form itself.

Rebecah can dance, and feel the beat through the vibration of the floor and to some extent through her hearing aids. Hearing impairment does not impede dance, neither does restricted language. Who's to say that something very special couldn't arise from her ability to do this?

And so, in being prepared to push back boundaries and saying 'yes' to things, I never know in which direction they will take me. It was in saying 'yes' to writing this book that so much has been revealed to me as I formulate my experiences into the written word.

An Exotic Adventure

THERE IS A HARVESTING OF SOULS, AN END OF TIMES, A FINALE, to our great adventure here on earth, and it is happening now: '...the harvest is the end of the world; and the reapers are the angels,' Matthew 13:39. Perhaps this is true, perhaps symbolic.

As the plane touched down in Malaysia, the sun was massive and brilliant orange in colour, casting an exotic hue over the jungle and adding to the air of expectancy and excitement. This was to be a great adventure for both Rebecah and myself.

As we alighted from the plane, the darkness and humidity engulfed us and sweat began pouring from our pores. It was exciting but cloying, and I felt I couldn't breathe. I never really did adjust to the humidity, but it was something I learned to live with. Our first night in the hotel was something of a shock. Belying the splendid façade it was a relic from a former imperial past. There were four-poster beds of rusty metal, cockroaches, and tardy waiters. The place hadn't seen a lick of paint or anything resembling it, and as for general cleanliness, well, the sheets were clean; I wouldn't vouch for the mattresses. The best course of action was one of surrender, and of imbibing something of the atmosphere, past and present and this we could enjoy.

Rebecah wished to savour the delights of KL and so my first port of call was a temple in the heart of the rural Indian community. I journeyed with a newly found companion, Stuart. We were not disappointed at what we saw. Such things as I shall describe to you I had only heard about, though they are widely known. A young priest was presiding over the events, and from what I could discern he had a huge responsibility. Men and women, mostly young, and in an hypnotic state, were having pins stuck in their tongues, or long poles, about one inch in diameter and possibly eight feet long, inserted into their cheeks. Others were having sharp metal hooks put in their chests, with limes on the ends, and yet others were carrying huge metal frames adorned with flowers called kavadis.

Each person had an entourage of 'assistants' whose task it was to encourage and keep in their hypnotic state with chanting and clapping. Had some of them moved out of this trance-like state, they could not have closed their mouths or brought their tongue back to facilitate swallowing, because of what was inserted into their tongues or cheeks, to mention nothing of the injury and pain incurred. The priest needed to be able to assess whether they were in the right state to take this otherwise life threatening abuse of their bodies. One man was nodding his head, demanding that more things be 'poked' into him and the priest was – rightly, in my opinion – refusing, and I could sense the disappointment.

Some of them walked about a mile, and again the priest had to be there to receive them at their destination, to place sacred ash on the areas where things had been removed and to make sure that their recovery was successful. People took some time to recover from such an ordeal; yet, miraculously, there was little blood, and healing was almost instant. I marvelled at how they could do such things and wondered what was so different about their culture and psyche from my own. I was to have something of a taster...

We ventured over to another area where we encountered more brave souls walking on hot coals. It was difficult to see and I became separated from Stuart. I found myself being pressed against lots of strange, sweaty bodies and felt distinctly uncomfortable. I immediately extricated myself from the situation to find Stuart, but alas, was unable to get close enough to witness the procedures. This, however, turned out to be fortuitous, because as we turned to walk away we came face to face with a tall, blond European who was eying us most pointedly. Being the only 'white' faces around, there was a natural empathy that one experiences when in non-familiar surroundings. The three of us ventured over to an open-air restaurant and enjoyed an evening meal together.

It turned out that he organised fire-walking sessions, particularly for Europeans, who didn't necessarily subscribe to any religious doctrine, but who wondered, like myself, how such things were achievable and what processes were entailed in achieving them. We agreed to meet our new-found Australian friend, Carrie, the next day in a small house with a private back garden on the edge of the town. Rebecah joined me later that evening.

Rebecah and I arrived the next day to find it full of Europeans, all searching, like ourselves, for a more enlightened state of existence, or just after excitement. Rebecah was particularly excited about this venture. I wondered if anyone there had the same specific quest as me. I would wait to see. Carrie seemed to home in on Rebecah in a special way.

Before the afternoon's procedures were underway, whilst exchanging preliminary pleasantries, a rat type creature appeared in the living room area where we were all sitting or lying. Some were on the floor and a couple of the women made a hasty leap on to the chairs, but that didn't help as rats can climb. There were shrieks and general pandemonium, but it didn't end there. Two more seemed to appear from nowhere, followed by a fourth. Most of us decided to remain cool, but it was Carrie who actually took things in hand and hurried outside in search of boxes. Soon everyone was scurrying round the house looking for these creatures and covering each with a box weighted down with a few books.

The scene was quite hilarious, I can tell you, with squeaking, moving boxes dotted around the house. Plan B involved the successful manoeuvre of these creatures outside. Three of them were easy, but one escaped. It headed for the 'coolest dood in town', the one who had no problem with any of this! He turned and ran the other way and the rat seemed to follow him. Everyone howled.

I made my way into the bathroom, but couldn't find the light. Being barefooted was the norm in these parts, and I felt something warm and soft under my foot. I screamed and someone turned on the light. Fortunately I had managed to sidestep this 'gooey thing' without lending my full weight to rest. There, seemingly staring up at me, was the ugliest bulbous greeny/multicoloured toad you ever did see! Now, I *hate* toads. Give me rats and cockroaches any day, but amphibians and reptiles repulse me. It could have been poisonous, I wasn't sure, but I wished it well away from me. It didn't turn into a prince, that's for sure, and dutifully disappeared down an open drain – from whence it came.

When it was out of the way, you'd reckon that that would have been the end of it now, wouldn't you just... Recovering a few moments later with a nice cup of tea in hand, what do you suppose plopped into it? A little lizard, which had momentarily lost its grip from the ceiling, just at exactly the point where I was holding my cup. I surmised that its plight was worse than mine.

Preparations for the evening's fire-walking began in earnest. Carrie was quite intense and serious about his work and lit beautiful joss sticks here and there to set the atmosphere. It worked for me. Immediately I felt a long-lost affinity with some kind of heightened experience, which had as yet evaded me, when I smelt them. Simply put, those joss sticks certainly put me into a spiritual state of mind. After twenty minutes or so meditating, Carrie began to read some uplifting words which I don't remember, but which had a soothing effect. Rebecah let the whole event wash over her and was content to imbibe. He then put us into pairs and there began a feet washing ceremony with water and a little herb essence, where we took it in turns to caress each other's feet, talking to them as we washed and expressing gratitude to them for their service. He likened our feet, providing a steadfast service to our bodies, to our human form, providing service to our 'oversouls', as he called them.

The philosophy, the words, didn't matter to me. Was what was taking place here enough to somehow convince our minds that we wouldn't get burnt when walking across the hot coals? Was it altering our consciousness in a way that was possibly unperceived by us? He told us, of course, that we'd be fine, that we'd experience from this what we needed to experience and that everything was 'in divine order'. He told us repeatedly that we would not get burnt and walked over the coals slowly, many times, to prove the point.

I had decided that this was only a sidestep to my main purpose on this journey, and that walking on these coals would take me no further along my inner path to enlightenment; the Indians had proved that. It hadn't turned them into gurus. I wasn't trying to appease the gods like them, either, and if facing my fears was what it was all about, I'd done that in the bathroom! Internal dialogue could convince me of anything.

Alice, a young girl, had said that she knew I was going to do it. Did I believe her? But then I watched Rebecah do it. Rebecah had shared the feet-washing ceremony as my partner, which was beautiful, but we had exchanged little in the way of language. She had heard virtually nothing of the hype, or the spiritual preamble, and yet she had imbibed everything! Her achievement set me thinking and gave me more serious food for thought. Here she was, one of the first to run across.

'Well done, Rebecah!' was my delighted exclamation, as she jumped and danced around for joy. 'Any burns?'

'No, none,' was her reply, accompanied with a big grin and a great sense of achievement. Then in walked a teenage boy, new to the whole idea. He knew what was happening and immediately walked across. It was enough that Rebecah had imbibed the energy of the spiritual exchange without the words, but here was someone who hadn't done either. Perhaps it was enough for him to have made an internal commitment prior to his arrival.

There were two of us left who hadn't walked across. I had watched a young woman psyche herself up to go, and go she did. I'd never expected it of her. Right, so if these people are not burning themselves, then what can be so different about me? I reasoned. Then, poised with an intention to 'go', I went. Something inside me – or was it outside? – propelled me forward. I can almost relive the experience now as I write about it.

Unbelievable! The coals didn't even feel hot. I was doing the impossible and on completion (and I ran) I felt no pain. Was I imagining it? No pain! It was exhilarating. Now I felt as though I was in an altered state of consciousness. I did it again; same result. I decided not to try a third time in case the magic wore off.

This proved to me one thing; that we go into altered states of consciousness far more often and more easily than we realise. If we are not aware of it and something like this can be achieved, then what is really going on around us that is unknown to us? My thoughts turned again to that young boy who came to join us late, the son of a couple who were there and who also, I reminded myself, hadn't had any of the preambles we'd had. He simply walked across. Was his subconscious working on him before he came, was he tapping into something we had created, or is it easy just to switch the mind quickly by a sheer act of will? Ordinarily, if he – or anyone else – had put a foot on those embers they would have burnt it, that's for sure.

In the aftermath, there were some with painful blisters. As for myself, nothing, not a thing. No buckets of cold water were necessary for me. Rebecah reminded me that she had two small blisters in the same place on each foot. They were, according to Carrie, to do with the feminine side of her being, which now needed attention. Rebecah agreed.

I felt proud of myself for ages after that. This had been something; an initiation of sorts, and a valuable part of my journey, I realised, but I needed to plough on with my life's intent. I needed to know something, completely, with my 'knowing', and nothing less would satisfy me.

Rebecah had her own reasons for making the journey. She wanted to see where she was born and reconnect with the places which weren't even in her conscious memory. Her sense of adventure was a dominating force.

That night, before I slept, I glanced out of the windows at the stars, not with a romanticised wonder, but with an emptiness at not knowing the mystery of it all. I brought to mind a poem, written by a friend of my father's, Herbert Whone:

> Twinkle twinkle, little star,
> How I wonder what you are –
> Perhaps one day I'll know inside
> Without a ten-year rocket ride.

I wanted to know inside. I had acquired, if you like, certain pieces of a picture, and I knew what inspired me, what set up an inner resonance, and I was going to find the bigger picture. I *was* going to find it, and not be persuaded by others. In the past I had paid a heavy price for such determination and was only reprieved in the final hour. However, that part of the story was behind me. For now, I shall continue with events as they unfolded.

Following My Trail

IT IS NOT MY TASK, NOR MY DESIRE, TO BEGIN A BELIEF SYSTEM, especially as I don't know any more than anyone else. Besides which, I don't really have one, as any beliefs I have are constantly knocked on the head and overturned. My writing here is as much for my own benefit as for other people's, and it is in the telling of my story that I learn so much myself. If sharing my life with others brings some happiness, or some food for thought, that is a wonderful bonus. In all honesty, I am excited about the thought of other people possibly reading my story, and I don't know what outcomes will ensue, if any; and that too is part of the fun.

It was the external and internal trail I was in search of, not the physical path but the inner path on an outward journey. During my life, I have looked into religion and found truths in all the different teachings, but no organised religion or practising doctrine of any kind has ever appealed to me; too many externals, too many rules; not for me, not this time around. I did, however, make an exception to my inner rule prior to this time, and this was when I paid a heavy price, as mentioned earlier. I was prepared to stay with a sect of people and surrender to their doctrine in order to attempt to move further towards gaining enlightenment for an indeterminate amount of time. This was a mistake, if there are such things.

The Christ figure, as presented in the Bible and taught in Sunday school, has always held a special place in my heart. I still, even now, think of Him as 'gentle Jesus, meek and mild'. How much of the story itself is actually true was becoming irrelevant.

It is this childlike quality within me that has enabled me to know my truth, to be discerning and to lift my vibration and make my heart sing. Measuring truth by any other criteria has got me into trouble. I had come on this journey with only the merest inkling that somebody here existed who could help me, and I didn't know how, if at all, I was going to access that person. It was trust on what would seem an absurd level, although, in the light of my previous experience, I knew that even if I found such a person I wouldn't be with him for long, but my heart resonated so deeply with what I had heard that my journey was not even an option.

I needed to trust that whatever happened to me and to Rebecah was part of the overall plan, even though I couldn't make the connection for myself. This opened the two of us to all kinds of experiences.

Carrie, myself, Rebecah – where we could include her – and a handful of the 'walking on coals' group had talked well into the night. There were a couple of 'chanellers' amongst them. In yesterday's terms they would have been known as 'mediums'. My initial reaction to such people was one of awe and trust. I have since learned to be wary and very, very discerning.

Helena was someone I had met within the group and had been attracted to. She was a chaneller, but was actually sceptical about her own gift. Her ability at 'channelling' was appealing to me for many sound reasons, and I had enormous trust for what she brought forward, yet still stood back to discern my own truth. Always, I had learnt to do this. Helena channelled without going into trance, or becoming pious or weird in any way. She had a healthy scepticism for anything that didn't sit right with her own instincts and didn't feel in any way superior to others; in fact she considered the gift something of a burden and had to be persuaded to use it, often requiring proof or confirmation that she was on the right track. That combination of factors was healthy as far as I was concerned. So now I will relate our episodes in the temple, which transpired as a result of her direction, through channelling.

Helena and myself decided to do one or two things together, whilst Rebecah stayed with friends. We had, as our initial focus, a certain temple, which had a strong energy. It was a good place to start, especially since Helena had been guided to go there.

We were all to stand in the grounds of the temple, in allocated spots, where we were mere conduits of energy and focus, whilst Helena herself allowed her mind to soar, and in this case, connect with the planet of Venus, and the goddess of that name. Venus represented the feminine love energy, for which this temple had originally been dedicated, though the knowledge of this had, according to her, been lost. Apparently some of the early temples, and sites on which later temples and churches were built, were balanced between male and female energies as the original idea was a Father-Mother god in one, and that balance had become imbalanced and male dominated. The balance needed redressing. On occasions like this I had to just allow the process to happen, as I didn't have a clue about such things, and trusted the integrity of those doing the work. My own intentions were in the right place, I knew that.

What Helena did on this occasion was not to talk but to bring the energy down, through her chakra system (the vortexes of energy within the body) and, by thought intent, channel it into sugared pills which had been left soaking in alcohol. (This, I'm told by my sister, who is a homeopath, is a simplified version of how homeopathic remedies are made; and indeed, a mutual friend of ours is producing planetary remedies and I can tell you they have a very profound and lasting effect, similar to the one I am about to describe now.)

We both took these pills and the effect for us was both quick and profound. For myself the effect kicked in within minutes of taking the pill; just one pill, that's all it needed. I felt good inside; a sense of well-being enveloped me. The things that would normally have an emotional pull on me ceased to do so, and I was somehow above the negative effects of those around me. For the next few days I could feel happy doing whatever I was doing; there was no sense of boredom with the otherwise mundane; in fact, everything I was doing gave me a strong sense of being present in my body, and that was connected to my higher purpose and was therefore meaningful. There was an underlying excitement to all this.

I gained a new insight into the meaning of the inner child. It was that connection within me to who I really am, and I wasn't caught up with the many 'I musts'. A realisation dawned that the 'I musts' come in many guises: logic, emotion, all fear-based thinking, which is not who we are and which distracts us from being who we are. I didn't have a craving for chocolate or any food but vegetables, and it was easy to stick to this. I was more in tune with my body's real requirements, but I wasn't having to deny myself foods. What I *did* desire to eat felt good and my body felt lighter. Lastly and very importantly for me, my energy levels increased. That was something of a miracle, as I was always tired. (The desire to eat only vegetables, however, didn't last.) So, Venus and Helena, thank you. Wow!

One more thing is worth a mention here. I felt a greater connection to something that I perceived as being *outside* myself, yet the connection was made from *within* myself. This was a bit like falling in love with someone you haven't met. It was exciting because as far as I was concerned, a huge step had taken me closer to what I had always wanted: 'ascension' – whatever that meant – or to put it more simply, the ability to access higher dimensions without dying. This trusting the process lark was indeed paying off, at this stage.

It is at this point in the juncture that I need to share the incident which shook me to my core and for which I paid that heavy price, nearly losing everything, my family and sanity; because with hindsight, I wouldn't have been so easily able to make that leap in awareness, had it not happened. Here it is.

About a year prior to this, I had decided to join a spiritual group in America. The people there, as it turned out, no longer carried in their experience the essence of the true teachings through not understanding on a conscious enough level. I had listened to their rhetoric and had become intellectually convinced that their methods could move me towards enlightenment. A long battle ensued between my heart and my head. I threw in my part-time jobs teaching music, too. My head – or more appropriately, my ego – won the battle, despite those around me telling me it was suicide. Whilst out there I began to experience panic attacks, as well as what can only be described as seething emotional pain at leaving my husband, who by this time was angry and distraught. This was largely because my return was indeterminate.

When I arrived on campus, I knew it was a mistake. My heart sank and continued to sink to the depths of despair. The leader had died and things were degenerating, with competition for leadership and egos flying high. The situation was dire. People fought for control, egos ruling egos, the blind leading the blind and everything an utter shambles.

The suffering was immense, whilst people convinced themselves, as I was doing, of the 'truth' of something their hearts told them was all a lie. To have given up everything and invested in a lie was more than they could bear too. (Of course, there *was* an essence of truth in the original teachings, but they weren't perceived at a self-realised level, so it became the equivalent of religious fervour and rules, people telling others what to do – minus the violence, though I've even heard reports since of that, too.)

I returned home in the nick of time to save my marriage. A lesser man would have kicked me into touch well before that. However, the assault on my system was so severe that somehow my body/mind/spirit couldn't cope and I began having the experience of being 'beside myself'. We don't use these hand-me-down expressions for nothing, so whoever came up with that one must have had the experience. I was terrified. I couldn't get back into myself, and had thoughts of being like it for the rest of my life, perhaps in a mental asylum, drugged up. I couldn't function. At its most severe I somehow managed to get in a car and see my friend Mark. Mark said that he didn't know how I got there and thought I was going to die. I felt that if I'd died in that state, I would have lost my soul.

Mark was and is a psychic and a healer. He saved my bacon. He used his healing skills, moving energies around my head and 'third eye' area. I was fortunate that he had in his collection a huge piece of volcanic rock called haematite, which was placed at my feet. Immediately I could feel 'me' slowly returning into myself. I took this life-saving rock home and even slept with it. After about two weeks and a couple more 'Mark' visits, I was more or less back to normal, but was to experience 'shaky moments' until up to one year afterwards. Mark well knows how I feel about him and his willingness to help me.

Mark, and others like him, often go unheralded and unheeded

today, and it is a great shame. He will have his day, but meanwhile, like so many people, he struggles on, and those with the 'official' stamp of approval can legally drug us up. (This is not meant to be insulting to the medical profession, but there could, I feel sure, be some alternatives to drugs.)

Although I didn't cry much during this whole episode, it was the worst experience of my life, worse than the discovery of Rebecah's deafness, because of the sheer fear factor. To try to summarise this, it was like bereavement in a fear-based void, without hope. Fortunately for me, and unlike many in the history of humanity, it was relatively short-lived.

Stuart turned to Rebecah for help. She could literally feel her heart being tugged when he was with her, but didn't really know how to help, except by being kind. James had made a firm declaration to himself to be around for his dad as much as possible. Neither of my children, both at university at the time, wanted me to leave, but understood my deeper needs. I know that James struggled to come to the realisation that I could be wrong. It was my sister who was instrumental in finally pulling us all back together, and I'm eternally grateful to her, too. Sometimes, when the time is right, we have to down tools and help, or even interfere...

However, what this taught me was very simple: I needed to get out of my head and into my knowing, or my heart. Thinking and logic have got us where we are today, and we're in a mess. I needed to experience, first hand, the danger of this. I also realise, in writing this, that it was *me* who gave myself the experience. Also, the fact that it was so severe was something I needed too, because I wasn't understanding the futility and seriousness of how the thinking process takes us away from who we really are. It takes us away from functioning as we are meant to function, I believe.

There is a wonderful book by Ekhart Tolle called *The Power of Now*. I shall quote from it now, as it demonstrates so admirably what I wish to say.

> I don't want to lose my ability to analyse and discriminate. I wouldn't mind learning to think more clearly, in a more focused way, but I don't want to lose my mind. The gift of thought is the most precious thing we have. Without it we would just be another species of animal...
>
> The predominance of mind is no more than a stage in the evolution of consciousness. We need to go on to the next stage now as a matter of urgency, otherwise we will be destroyed by the mind, which has grown into a monster...
>
> Enlightenment means rising above thought, not falling back to a level below thought, the level of an animal or a plant. In the enlightened state, you still use your thinking mind when needed, but in a much more focused and effective way than before. You use it mostly for practical purposes but you are free of the involuntary internal dialogue, and there is inner stillness. When you do use your mind and particularly when a creative solution is needed, you oscillate every few minutes or so between thought and stillness, between mind and no mind. No mind is consciousness without thought. Only in that way is it possible to think creatively, because only in that way does thought have any real power. Thought alone, when it is no longer connected with the vast realm of consciousness, quickly becomes barren, insane, destructive...

This may sound rather intellectual, and I am not able to fully experience what he is saying, not being enlightened myself, but consider this: huge wars are created on the back of an ethos, an ideal, a religious or political conviction; but if the love of God were actually experienced, there would be no need for any of that, and at the very least, there would be harmony in diversity.

Tolle describes something else which also beautifully characterises the state I was in:

> Are you stressed? Are you so busy getting to the future that the present is reduced to a means of getting there? Stress is caused by being 'here' and wanting to be 'there', or being in the present but wanting to be in the future. It's a split that tears you apart inside. To create and live with such an inner split is insane. The fact that everyone else is doing it doesn't make it any less insane...

To return to my story, it was after experiencing this episode in the temple that I was able to continue my journey with even greater impetus, and certainly more physical stamina. The whole episode also brought to mind the words of Ekhart Tolle, and so a new creation was born in me, in the form of two poems, which I wrote that evening and subsequently shared with Helena. Not surprisingly, the first one is called, 'Thinking'. Here it is:

Thinking

Give full attention to all that you do
Internal chatter is not really you.
It blocks who you are, so do not pursue
Stop thinking so peace and joy can shine through.

It's not what you do but how,
Being focused on the quality of now.
So be firm with yourself and vow
To be present, let the real you, allow.

Thinking has become a real affliction
It controls us, feeds us severe addiction;
But when you're present you raise your vibration
Bringing quality to each situation.

We believe that thinking serves our need
Doing the crossword – just more mind to feed,
But it's in presence that we actually lead
Because our soul can now serve as we've truly been freed.

Source

Source is the place we must choose to be
As it's only from there we can truly see,
Not with the eye looking forward from past,
Not with the future I; perception won't last,
But in Now, in the stillness, in peace and beyond
Where one touches creation and holds that firm bond.

It's from Source where creation has any real power,
It's from Source where the greatest ideas will flower,
It's Source that's in now, and not in the mind,
The key to be liberated, your real self to find,
Not with ongoing dramas to identify,
But fully present and focused, the real inner I (eye).

The real I is Source and is one with all things,
The small boy, the Arab, the Angel with wings,
The you and the me and the 'all that there is';
The outpouring of love in that presence to live,
Not love on the outside but love of the self,
For true self is Source and gives infinite wealth.

Mind is only one step in man's evolution,
But it's time to move on, create a new revolution.
Compulsive thinking has gone beyond sense,
We need now to free ourselves, make matters less dense.
All our great teachers, inventers, knew how
To exist in the moment, being present in Now.

The Christ and the Buddha, Einstein and Mozart
Were in touch with the Source where perception is sought.
It matters not whether 'tis science or art:
Creation is drawn from that infinite part
Of our being, in Source; for this is what's sane –
Not perpetual mind patterns again and again.

So watch your thoughts like a cinema show
Don't attach, just see them come and go.
The body feels emotion in every cell;
Feel them, release them, on thoughts do not dwell,
Then let those gaps within the mind
Feel peaceful, to yourself be kind,
Until they expand your universe
And fill your whole being with both heaven and earth.

Onwards Towards our Destination

REBECAH WAS A STALWART COMPANION. SHE DIDN'T, HOWEVER, wish to read my poetry or partake of the more esoteric part in my life, unless the experience was physical, like the walking on coals. I freely gave her a ticket of leave to find where her own joys lay. Certainly at this stage in her life she was – and still is – ambitious, but her African experience had left her with a determination for that ambition to include deaf people, so that she was not too far out of her comfort zone. She had been out on a limb, and was finding the necessity to reel in a little, so to speak.

There was a mutual understanding that neither one of us would ever take offence, which allowed each of us the potential to explore whatever avenues presented themselves, either independently or together. The relationship was, of course, still mother and daughter, and she hated the repeated references to our being like 'sisters'. Yet such familiarity didn't breed contempt, as we always maintained a common respect and indeed a love for each other. We shared similar interests too, apart from the esoteric. There was a love of beauty, good food and posh hotels, architecture, home decor, nature, and, of course, people – and we could laugh together: very important! One of our best times was spent at Club Med, where we mutually partook of many of the activities, not least of which was dancing.

I left Rebecah in the safe hands of friends for a sojourn up in the mountains with Helena and another companion we'd met of like mind called Louis. My intent was to seek out this guru and see if indeed he possessed great love and wisdom. We only spent three days together but as we travelled, each experiencing our own growth as people, our personalities – fundamentally quite different – began to be more overshadowed by our soul, so the commonality of thought and desire merged more and more as our journey continued. Helena brought with her much that was of interest and value into our lives. The three of us melded most admirably. The mountain pass, however, proved to be quite an ordeal for me, and our taxi made several stops, which allowed me to relieve the contents of my stomach, as well as trying to heave up what was no longer there.

Halfway, or thereabouts, we stopped at a fairly basic café set into the mountain side, and were able to enjoy spectacular views. Helena was sitting opposite us, devouring a succulent piece of pineapple, when we saw her lower jaw gradually descend. As Louis and I lifted and turned our heads, approaching us was a pigmy, scantily clad and carrying a long bamboo cane, which turned out to be a blowpipe for shooting poisoned arrows at wild boar. He spoke minimal English, but the gist was that he wanted us to buy the pipe.

It was an interesting episode. The man had presence, and courage too, to approach the tourists as he did. In height, he probably didn't exceed three feet six inches and in looks he was something akin to the Australian Aborigine, but not quite. When presented with a situation such as the one I'm describing here, it is quite a task to cash in on the full extent of what is happening. Here was possibly a human relic from a bygone age, still living in his native habitat, the tropical jungle, there for us to see; touch, if we dared and could get his permission; smell, though I didn't notice a smell; and just generally experience. We couldn't do much in the short time we had available, and it wasn't our intention to go into the jungle to find out more, so we each experienced the moment in our own way.

For myself, I can almost sense the man as I stand here writing this. I wonder if he has since died and is tuning in to me. I have a feeling of love, of a sense of harmony and inner gentleness. There is perhaps also a sense of regret that these peoples have now been absorbed into the general populace and their way of life lost. Yes, I'm sure that he wanted to convey these things. As I write now I am asking in my mind if there is anything else that he wishes me to convey. He said that we had planned our meeting prior to incarnation, and that he was more aware of my being than I was of his. True!

Salamat! Peace to the world! Peace, peace, and living in harmony with nature, is the message I'm getting. He's joining forces now with other earth native tribal peoples, and I am feeling overwhelmed; tears are beginning to run down my face. I must stop writing now and be in harmony with them for a moment.

It is not long since that I threw that blowpipe away. I appreciated it and what it represented, but as in all things there is a time and a purpose. I'm told that most if not all the pigmies of Malaysia have become absorbed into the community and many have intermarried. Apparently some of them have reached lawyer status, which may make an interesting anthropological study. I honestly wouldn't know how knowledge of this would fit into current theories. It seems to me that the phenomenon we call intelligence is fairly evenly distributed throughout all races, but that other factors which go to make up our inner constitution are not. For example, alcohol has had a very detrimental effect on the Native American Indians, but certain natural drugs from plants seemed to have enhanced their lives.

And so that moment in the café passed and we continued with our journey. Our destination was to be a 'ye olde' English-style colonial cottage set among the tea plantations, within rolling descending mountains and spectacular views. It had been procured for us as a special favour, by a friend of a friend. It was perfect. The weather was decidedly cooler, and I felt that I could breathe again, which was a blessing. In fact, we actually felt a little cold!

We arrived at the cottage only to find that the internal accommodation was really quite basic, but that bothered us not one jot. We had decided to eat out, as it was so cheap. There's always something special about eating in the open air, lingering over a coffee or a glass of wine. It's something you rarely get to do in England.

As we walked back to the cottage on that first evening, Helena began to open up about some of the work she was doing within the business world, back in Canada. If I were to put her work into some kind of category, which of course, it isn't, I would label it 'spiritual psychology'.

She talked about teaching people to create win-win situations where everyone got the best they could out of any deal, whether this be policies within a company or dealings with another company. To attain this state of harmony meant people looking to change themselves, rather than try to change others. How this inner state of change was tackled was interesting.

She said that we all have a window from which we view things and that that window is influenced by our attitudes, opinions and belief systems, which become hardened into our own subjective truths, and very early on, too; often as young as eight years of age. From these perspectives we judge both ourselves and others, which results in not accepting those outside our parameters, and placing limitations on what we ourselves can achieve, if we have to stay within them. Very often a belief system will go unchallenged until a crisis arises in our lives, forcing us to look at the way we view things and our tolerance level towards others.

What was really interesting for me was that certain salesmen in one particular company were given both favourable and unfavourable conditions in which to work, and in every case the successful ones eventually continued their success, and similarly, the failures perpetuated their failures, proving – to me, at any rate – that our state of being is determined by us, not external circumstances. Of course, I'm talking here about similar areas within one country, not the Third World, where situations can be intolerable.

This state of success, or not, is in turn determined by our 'comfort zone', and how far we are willing to extend it. If we stay within it, we keep those limitations. That ceiling, or level to which we each aspire, is achievable in small steps, and any large step could result in us landing with a painful crash. So, we go from machine operator to MD one step at a time, but we can hold our vision. (How I had learned that lesson!)

She concluded by saying that money is a big issue for most people. I interjected at this point with something I had experienced in my hometown. It was known as LETS, which stands for 'local exchange trading systems'. It involves sharing skills or swapping favours within a community using an invented currency. For example, the plumber mends my washing machine, I sew Jo's curtains and Jo does the plumber's accounts. The thought of appreciating each other, equally, was appealing to me, too. Besides, it would dispel the notion that you have to do as little as you can for as much money as you can get. This, she confirmed, would be a huge step forward in itself, because most people had the unconscious understanding that they did have to give the least amount of money for the maximum benefit, or the minimum work for the most amount of money. People also have the notion that there's not enough to go round, and that someone else having something necessitates their being denied it, which is also a fallacy. Need, not greed, would summarise that one.

We talked into the night, Louis adding bits about taking responsibility for our lives and not being a victim. We all needed to take responsibility for our lives at that point and get some sleep, for tomorrow was another day and we didn't want to sleep it away.

It was light at about 7 a.m. and quite cool. I wondered what the day would bring. A few yards away I could hear the sound of water tinkling its way down the mountain side. It reminded me of my home in England on a cloudy, drizzly day with the sound of the waterfall audible from my bedroom. However, I wasn't in England, not with my physical body, and my focus quickly turned to the present moment and my goal there.

As I lay in bed, I wondered too why, here in the East, with its long tradition of spiritual practice, so few of the people that I'd met had broken free of their traditions and gone beyond them to really look at the essence of truth. The same was true everywhere, but in the West there were those few who had a greater willingness to open to other possibilities. I knew that they must have been around, and that I was not part of their network as I would be at home, but even so it was disappointing to me to notice how few there were. I thought the law of attraction, and like attracting like, would have worked its charm more than it had.

In the West I had met many people, though few relative to the general population, who were willing to look deeper into themselves, or into the realms of the paranormal, to try to find out who they really were, why they were here on this planet and where they had come from.

No orthodox views or scientific evidence, at least that which we are allowed to see, has satisfied this quest for me. It's been disappointing and frustrating at times, too, and at least once, downright dangerous, as I wrote earlier; but it's never been boring. There was always an underlying excitement to all this, and there's something else too: there's always that inner connection to that higher force. It has been really strong since taking those 'channelled sugar pills', and has never really left, ever, and I experience it as a powerful force down the centre of my body. I'm sure too that I knew all of this long, long before I was born, but the forgetting has sent me on so many interesting and exciting adventures, of which this story I am writing now is a part.

My search has led me down so many avenues, all connected at the top, like a huge pyramid, but all so varied and exciting, when experienced at this level, separately. I have read many spellbinding and uplifting books; I have sat in mediumistic circles, and taken part in different types of healing, sometimes with spectacular results, too. I have looked at the sacred geometry connecting buildings in major cities, connecting sacred sights around the world, planets and our own bodies. I have read about, and experienced inwardly, extraterrestrials and UFOs, I have seen auric photography, chakra photography, taken photographs which, when developed, have shown evidence of gnomes, fairies and on one occasion, an Indian Chief. I have been to many churches to look at the evidence of real knowledge hidden within them, Roslyn Chapel, near Edinburgh, being a shining example. I have felt the presence of the Holy Grail around the chalice well in Glastonbury, and so many more things that I haven't even touched upon here. And all the time this outward journey goes on, so does the inward one. I have had to face many fears and learn to let go and surrender to many things. The more I've let go, the freer I have become.

Not for me the life of the aesthetic, shutting out the world in order to become enlightened, but a balance, a balance, always a balance, between the spiritual and the earthly. This balance has meant being able to be appropriate, wearing the different mantels of mother, wife and teacher, showing love and compassion – especially to irritating relatives – and yet being detached. It is not easy being human. I remember attending the funeral of a Buddhist friend of mine, and the words of the addresser, which I do not recall exactly, were, that if we were to take all the beings in all the universes to represent the size of our bodies, then those willing to come to earth would represent the tiniest dot on your thumbnail, such was the toughness of it, or something like that. I remember thinking that I hoped the rewards would be commensurate with the difficulty. I suspect that they are.

However, all these thoughts were taking me away from my focus. I put out the thought again. There must be someone out there who knew something of real value. As I was thinking that, there was a knock on my door. Louis walked in. I expressed a desire to go out and talk to a few people and see where – if anywhere – it might lead us. I had felt that we were guided to come up into mountains, so it was a matter of going deeply within to connect with our heartfelt intuition, to look for clues. We agreed to have an early morning pre-breakfast meditation. Helena could sometimes channel information through, and would do so if it felt appropriate.

Channelled information rarely came in the form of direct instruction about where to go or what to do, at least not for me and usually not for those with me, although some people are given information about which energy sites to visit, but these people can often intuit such things and have contracted to do them. For the remainder of us mortals, part of our journey is in learning to be in tune with ourselves and 'growing' enough to listen accurately to our own intuition. The answers come in the journey itself, rather than the final destination. Thus our outer and inner journey becomes one, which is as it should be.

Our Journey Intensifies

During our meditation a rather unusual thing happened: an African shaman came through. This was not to be our last contact with him, as I shall later relate. What was so different about this channelling was that there was a pungent smell accompanying his message; something in the order of aromatic herbs. It reminded me of burnt sage, which was traditionally used as a cleansing herb by some of the Native American Indians. Considering there was 'nothing' there, this was not only exciting, but also definite proof, if you like, of a presence.

This being was wise, and had had much in the way of experience on the earthly plane. He told us that if we wished to really open up to the higher realms our pituitary glands needed special attention. This was available to us but we needed guidance, which would also be available to us when the time was right. I knew what he was talking about. I knew it, I knew it precisely, and I didn't push the point any further because I knew also that this was in our hands. We had been given some information which I had suspected was true for a long time. It was tremendously exciting.

The second part of his message was fairly simple in its instruction, though more complex in its reasoning. We were to stay open and present in our thinking. That state of being created the right conditions for us to be guided to where we wished to be. Apparently, when we stay open the light force and thought energy flows through us, and we are not blocking this with our own thought processes, which are usually about the past or future. This we knew. What we didn't know was that staying in this state allowed for the activation of a third force. This could be felt as an energy when two people were in deep rapport; but apparently it was more than that, it was a creative force that came in to play which allowed things to 'happen', or our desires to be met. It was a 'law' within the universe. It was perceived as a 'law', but at the level of the infinite, actually there are no laws.

I thought back to my father and his insistence that the law of three was 'absolute'. He even painted three pictures, which he called a triptych, to illustrate the point. My husband too studied this law, mathematically. For myself, I had no desire whatsoever to understand this with my head, or my logic, as you might say. Only my experience counted. I was reminded too of being in a classroom when I had asked the children to draw with a pencil compass within a circle. When they coloured in the drawings, I found myself insisting that the children use only three colours and I didn't really know why. When they kept to three colours the results were often spectacular – almost 'other dimensional' – and could have been used as mandelas for meditation. When they added a fourth colour, their drawings became flat, however neat they were. This was my actual experience, but I couldn't get beyond it to the next level of understanding, or should I say, *feeling*, about it.

The children seemed to agree. In fact, one child – definitely an 'indigo child' – kept on drawing similar pictures at home and in his spare moments. He seemed to be captivated by them, which told me something, though I don't quite know what. It was to do with sacred geometry and his connection to higher things, I believe, and somehow the drawings he did took on the effect of being three-dimensional and therefore more meaningful to him. It gave me part of the picture but not all of it. Was this a curse, I asked myself, only getting part of the picture?

We'd decided to go into town, have a light breakfast and take a walk around some of the plantations, if we could find somewhere suitable. The town was scruffy and unkempt, but the local restaurants – if they could be called that – although basic and dirty by Western standards, sold delicious local meals and we'd never had any tummy upsets from any of them, which was surprising. I ordered a roti chanai, which was like a flaky pastry and unleavened bread rolled into one. There was some skill in making it, too. It was usually the men that cooked them; they would toss the dough in the air repeatedly to get the air in, and it was all done over a hot plate. Accompanying it was a simple vegetable curry sauce, and that would satisfy me till evening. It was delicious.

Helena ordered some toast and tea. I looked at her quizzically. Did she know something I didn't? She didn't explain the order at all. For some reason, Louis and I remained silent. Louis had ordered a yoghurt dish served on a banana skin with rice. Now rice was something that did not sit right with my palate, first thing in the morning. I think Louis was more acclimatised than me. Helena's 'breakfast' arrived. Just as I'd suspected, the tea was thickened with about half a tin of condensed milk and the toast was smeared in ghee and sprinkled with sugar. I glanced at Louis with a knowing nod, and suppressed a smile. We both chatted on as though nothing were amiss. Helena had never been to England, and I could feel the mischief surging within. She made a loud protestation, something like, 'Oh my goodness!' – but not quite. We continued the charade, asking her what was the matter. I suggested that perhaps she didn't like the ghee. The ghee was the least of it, and it was Helena's turn to look puzzled.

'Don't you have it like this in Canada?' I asked, innocently.

'What, you eat like this in England? You're joking!' It didn't take long for Helena to twig, as the banter became more and more ludicrous. It ended with my description of the Muslims only using their right hand when preparing food! Helena went without breakfast that day. We made it up to her with some roasted yams followed by a local fruit cocktail.

We found our walk and it was certainly picturesque. The countryside in our immediate environment was almost English in its flora and fauna and with its colonial houses dotted here and there. The hill sides were terraced and used mainly for growing vegetables. We saw the local women toiling away and exchanged a smile and universal 'Hello!' The cooler weather seemed to accommodate a greater variety of vegetables, many of which were taken down the mountain side and sold in the local markets. Further down the valley were rows and rows of tea bushes, now managed efficiently by the locals rather than the colonials.

We didn't chat much, but held that wonderful stillness within as we observed without. The pigmy again came to mind, and I stopped walking in order to feel the moment. As I looked but was not actually 'looking', my focus of attention being inward not outward, I noticed the land appear to shift and stretch, both to the right and to the left, as though I were drunk. It moved back again, then did it again. I decided not to share this slightly weird experience, but savour it and walk on. However, this experience was to continue with considerable regularity, and I began to feel what may have been happening. It was a shifting in dimensions around the earth, but beyond that I was unable to define it. At this stage, I wasn't sure. It also had something to do with the concept of time speeding up and the reaching of higher dimensions, but these thoughts were not formulated into any kind of discernable logic.

As we turned a corner we bumped into a young Indian man, handsome and aged about twenty-three. Walking with him was an auburn-haired, green-eyed, ebullient Irish girl. They each had a strong presence, and it came as something of a surprise to encounter two such people, out of the blue, so to speak, in this part of the world.

I immediately felt drawn to him. It was one of those feelings you get when you think you've known someone all your life. There was an instant rapport. I couldn't take my eyes off him. Apart from anything else, he was extraordinarily handsome; like a god incarnate, but the depth of love coming from his eyes – in fact from his whole being – was something else. Don't misunderstand me; I'm not attributing 'guru' status to him, but because I believe there's a God in all of us 'Hu-man (God-man) beings', the God within him was 'being' very apparent (as in an apparition). I love the etymology of words. I find that if it comes to my notice, then there's a message in there somewhere for me.

We introduced ourselves, and Sivara was his name. Well, that figured. He even had a godly name! Mariana, his friend, had us splitting our sides before long, but amidst all that the two of them pointed us in a very valuable direction. Sivara was on holiday with friends, but all Sivara's holidays had a spiritual quest, and so it was these friends that pointed him in the direction of the shaman. He had met up with Mariana 'perchance' and had agreed to help her, though he was to gain something from the experience himself.

Exciting Revelations

Mariana had come here for a holiday, just a holiday. It was only the second time she had flown and she hadn't enjoyed it the first time, but nothing prepared her for the ordeal this time around. The panic attack she experienced once the plane was taking off was severe enough to warrant sailing home, returning overland, or living there. None of those were viable options for obvious reasons, and naturally she wished to get back to her home in Ireland. She had spent the whole holiday looking for a cure for her phobia.

It turned out that the two of them had just been to visit an Afro-Indian shaman. It was quite a trek and the only way was by foot, at least from where we were situated now. They had stayed the night and we would have to do the same if we chose to walk from that point at that time.

We decided to venture back into town and share our stories and hopefully glean information on how to access this shaman, if indeed that's what we wanted to do. I was excited at spending more time with Sivara, anyway. I wondered if he felt that he'd known me in past lives, too. We found a posh, Western-style hotel where we could sit in the lap of luxury. It was still scruffy, but luxurious in comparison to everywhere else surrounding us. Sivara's opening remark did not disappoint me. Had we heard of 'Ishasarah?' he inquired, rather casually and dreamily.

We each reacted in our own ways, but nobody said anything. Sivara then looked pointedly at me and said, 'We're connected, aren't we?'

I hoped that everyone would remain silent so I could savour the moment. Sometimes speech can dissipate a certain magic. And now was magic. Mariana broke the spell.

'Jeez, that was awful, really awful! You never want to experience what I've just gone through! I mean it. 'Twas terrible noy. And I'll tell you what, I'd do it again tomorrow. I would that!'

'I thought it was terrible, Mariana,' said Sivara, laughingly and resignedly. He was obviously used to her. The rest of us nodded, smiled and waited for her to continue.

'Oh, 'twas indeed, so terrible. But how else can you find excitement like that? I'd go again tomorrow and the next day and the day after, but I don't think my mammy would approve.'

'Why not, Marie?' Helena asked.

'You can't have an orgasm like that with everyone watching, noy, can you? It's not right. I'm telling you noy, it's just not right, Stevie, is it?'

'It's *Sivara*.'

'That's what I said, isn't it? Noy, if you wish to go yourselves, you go along the track where we met, but if you do that, you'll be start'n from the wrong place! Then you walk along there for about two miles and you'll see a path leading to the right and that's a steep decline for about five miles. Have you got that, noy? Right, you got that, but if I were you I wouldn't go that way!'

I looked at Louis and Helena. They were by now holding their sides. Fortunately for me, they tackled her, which left me free to talk to Sivara. I encouraged him to be completely open, adding that I was pretty well getting the gist of things and that I knew about Ishasarah. This last piece of information put us both in the picture. You didn't search for the sort of knowledge unless you were seriously in earnest about your own inner life and the life of this planet, the two being intrinsically bound.

I looked straight into Sivara's eyes, and said, 'We were together in a life around two thousand years ago, weren't we? I think that I was an Essene in that lifetime, and it's my guess that you were too, or at least have imbibed one of their lives at soul level.' (The problem was I could never be certain about these feelings; not convinced, so to speak.)

On this last point Sivara was confused, but as for us both having been around in the same lifetime he heartily concurred. I clarified the last point by explaining that I had learned in Delores Cannon's books that people with soul permission could take on the memory of someone else's life, between incarnations, without actually having lived it, if it served both themselves and that of their soul group. She had discovered this with one of her clients during a deep hypnotic past life regression she was conducting. Other than that, Sivara didn't feel the necessity to delve any deeper, as it was the here and now that concerned us. As for myself, I always thought that this kind of information spoke of 'relative truths', that is, truth in accordance with the level of reality being experienced.

On practicalities, the way to reach this shaman was from a point of access a little further down the main road. From there it was only a two-mile rather than a seven-mile walk, hence the funny rhetoric from Mariana. The orgasmic experience she referred to was the process which involved the raising of the kundalini energy from the base of the spine and upward. This, according to Sivara, was only done very slightly, but the deep-rooted fears around her flying were not flying, so to speak, so it was deemed necessary. Mariana was hanging on to these fears, and she had done little in the way of meditation or work on herself in the past, so she needed powerful input. The shaman was well acquainted with such work and could go with her, in her mind, to reassure and guide her. The focus on raising the energy up from the base of the spine, causing the passing sexual experience, had been necessary, in order to free her mind from remaining rooted in earthly matters which were not telling her anything about her fears.

Sivara added as an aside that a little in the way of 'magic mushrooms' had been taken, or the process may have been a complete failure. This, he further clarified, was a safe procedure, providing it was done with guidance and love, and, of course, there were no side affects, or addictions, as with drugs. As for the experience itself, it was confidential, as I well knew, but whether it worked remained to be seen on Mariana's flight home. Sivara did volunteer another interesting factor. The shaman stood Mariana in a circle of protection which he physically drew on the earth around her. I have myself read about such things, but not actually experienced them. They hold an awesome curiosity for me.

I told Shivara what I had read and he in turn shared an actual experience, which I shall relate below, and which I found very exciting. I described what I had read. In the Middle East, around such places as Armenia and the Hindu Kush, there existed, apparently, wise men with magical powers. Around such folklore I associate the Whirling Dervishes, but I might be wrong. These people were capable of putting you in a circle without you being able to escape. Quite why they did it I'm not sure. Certainly it was to do with the power of the mind. Such people were bards, and carried ancient knowledge which they did not write down, but which had to be memorised. African shamans performed similar rituals in order to assist people in transcending their fears. One such example can be seen in a film called *The Power of One.* I looked at Sivara and asked him something which was in part rhetorical, as I'd spent some years working out the answer myself.

'Why, today, do we seem to have lost our mystics, witches, oracles, wise priests and priestesses? Why, when a child asked me in school, "Did God talk to Abraham and not us?" could I not answer?'

Sivara replied and I was heartened by his wisdom.

'I think many of our inherent psychic abilities have been deliberately bred out of us with the killing of such people as witches, for example, for the jealous power mongers that still exist today, and medical drugs, particularly vaccines, have also stifled us; dulled our minds in some way, not to mention food additives. In addition to this there might have been genetic interference to keep our own powers at bay, performed by those mentioned in all folklores. Hinduism and the Bible call them the gods, but they were probably extraterrestrials. Extraterrestrials were also the "voice of God". However, that was aeons ago, and at some level we had agreed that this would be *our* journey.'

It was Sivara's turn to share his experience. He had had a problem at school which his father believed was deeply psychological. Although a doctor, his father had had the wisdom to seek help from an old priest in India who had departed from tradition; a seer, if you like. The family had to wait for their holidays in England, and took off for India, where they still had some remaining relatives who would accommodate them.

Here follows the description of Sivara's experience. As a child, Sivara had a problem at school with one of the teachers, and no amount of medication or counselling cured the problem. The Indian 'seer' drew a circle of protection around him, and talked him down through a series of emotions, without perpetuating the cause for them. Eventually, with the help of the seer, Sivara reached a state of blackness and void. He cried and didn't like it, but then saw a pinprick of light come towards him, becoming brighter and brighter till it engulfed him, filling him with joy. From that state of joy, he returned to the teacher scenes, only to realise that the cause was nothing to do with what he was currently experiencing in his life but something which had occurred whilst he was a baby when his older sister had died. He had had to lie an unusually long time in the cot whilst his parents dealt with the trauma. The teacher had inadvertently made a comment about death, which had triggered an unconscious reaction from Sivara.

Surprisingly, on return to school after the treatment, the teacher's attitude changed dramatically – or was it that Sivara's attitude had changed? Sivara believed that this had worked so well because he had dealt with the cause from a state of joy, not misery, and not from a place where the problem was relived and perpetuated. (The reader can learn more about this from Brandon Bay's book, called simply *The Journey*, and a similar incident is enacted in a wonderful film mentioned earlier called *The Power of One*.)

We were all eager to know about Ishasarah, and Mariana had a passing interest, especially in the light of what she had received, so we were glued to Sivara's words during a second round of drinks.

The shaman, he said, knew about the knowledge of the ancients and was one of the few left on the earth today with such knowledge. He was now willing to break his avowed silence and share it. Here Sivara made a pregnant pause while we all waited with bated breath.

'This valuable and sacred knowledge or ancient secrets of the universe are of paramount importance to the planet at this time. So, your instincts were right. However, the Ishasarahs as a group no longer exist. In fact, truth to tell, I don't think that they ever really did. I think perhaps that you were all allured by the same information as me and as many of us from a book known as *Secrets of the Mountains*, subtitled, 'The Lost Ishas'. There are not many of us who would actually come out here to find them, and herein lies the point. It's something like *The Wizard of Oz* – seeking to find that which you had all along.'

I must have looked somewhat dejected, as did Helena and Louis, but Sivara continued.

'Don't worry; all is not lost, and there is a point to your being here and there are some surprises along the way. However, these will come from the shaman and not me. I would go now if I were you. I will see Mariana into a taxi and accompany you, if it is all right by you.'

It was great by us, and besides, we hadn't near finished with him yet!

We were about to visit someone whom I had hoped would be a remarkable person, and it was a rare opportunity indeed.

The Shaman

Inside the simple wooden house, which was more like a large hut, we all sat in a semicircle, facing him. As I looked at him and his eyes met mine, I was struck by something in his physical appearance. He was Afro-Asian. I remembered the channelling and the smell of the sage. The aroma of sage once again assailed our senses. Could it have been that this man consciously contacted us in the astral? I looked at him again, wondering if he was discerning my thoughts, but it did not feel appropriate to break the silence.

Something from deep within me stirred; something that I instinctively knew was connected to the bowels of the earth. My own guts were connecting with something from deep within the earth and coming up through me was a force, but I knew not what. It was as though I was giving birth. I felt very ill. My face clenched and I emitted a deep involuntary wail. I really and truly had no control over this. Not only did I feel ill, but that sense of abandon one has, when nothing matters, when you are about to give birth, was exactly how I felt. I would not have recognised that state of mind had I not given birth to my children. When Rebecah was born the pain was considerable, so I'd put that state of 'not caring' down to the pain. However, when James was born I had had an epidural and was not in pain, yet still experienced that same state of abandon. (I'm sure nearly all mothers worldwide will know exactly what I'm talking about. It wouldn't matter if the Queen walked in.)

We had been with the shaman for some considerable time, but this particular experience was unique to me and not at all what I had expected. The process was part of a deep cleansing. I had ingested some magic mushrooms which proved to be a poison to my system, so my body was having to cope with two things at once. I'd never taken any drugs (and never will), believing that this was damaging to my astral body and could set me back lifetimes. I had thought that the magic mushrooms would be fine, and indeed, the others *were* fine, but not I. A solid lesson had been imbibed here! However, I did see beautiful swirling colours, both pearlised and shimmering. I was also able to transmute any slightly negative images to fun ones or ones of beauty in an instant, with the quality of thought, namely love. None of the images seemed real, anyway.

I felt that at some level I may have been floating in higher dimensions, whatever that meant, and I noticed too the power of the spoken word and thought in such a state. Somebody, at one stage, mentioned the word fear, and I immediately had the feeling of being propelled rapidly down the dimensions and was back in the room with a jolt: not very pleasant! However, I cannot say that

I felt a closeness to Christ or God, or that I felt more of who I really was, or indeed, that I experienced a oneness with all that is. From this point of view the experience was disappointing. It was afterwards that I began to gain some perspective on the whole thing.

My inner knowing told me two things very clearly. Firstly, this: the here and now of this earthly experience was to be experienced fully, as it happened. This earthly, three-dimensional experience was soon to change, but until it did I was to be fully present with it, and that included all the emotional states. Any unpleasant experiences as well as the pleasant ones were to be felt and not avoided or buried, because only by doing this could I transmute the energies into a higher vibration. It was a matter of facing and clearing my fears. This is what I had agreed to do.

Secondly, and fantastic though this may sound (and believe me, it is difficult for me to own this inner knowing), I had agreed at some point in linear time, prior to birth, to specifically cleanse the earth in certain areas, along with many others who I know are doing a similar task. All this was to be done in accordance with divine law, in accordance with the agreed ascension of the planet. The ascension of the planet was something which the shaman knew about. This is the information I was searching for. This was the secret of the Ishasarahs.

The shaman spoke to us. The Ishasarahs were a myth, a story to encourage people to go within and find their truth. It was indeed something like *The Wizard of Oz* or the Holy Grail, pointing out the truth in disguise. The 'game' in this most limited and restricted world of ours was a bit like blind man's bluff. If the blindfold were removed, there would be no point in the game. The key was to actually *experience* the game. Yes the universe had worked with him to call us to him, to have certain experiences, but nobody was going to point the way; that was for us to discern, and more fool anyone who blindly followed the leadership of another.

He went on to say that everything evolves and has an allotted time span. The earth, a conscious, living, breathing entity, was evolving with or without us. The part we played within this process was a choice, but was largely made by soul agreement, as our time on earth with all its rounds or reincarnations was also coming to the end of its allotted span.

It was true that exciting and monumental things were happening on this planet and that if we could gain an overview we would be overwhelmed. We were, as he put it, 'going home'.

I was deeply moved by this statement because it brought to mind an experience I had had whilst on a meditation course. Everything around me became generally dark but was interspersed with blobs of yellow light. I was not afraid – in fact, anything but – rather more blissful than anything else, I would say. I had the feeling of being at home, totally loved and of never having been separate from that state; in fact there could be no other state, it was always so and any other state was not real. I shared my thoughts with the group and the shaman nodded knowingly. He added that from what he knew of his inner guidance what we were heading for was so much greater than even that. What a perfect way to end a day – but there was still a little more to come before our time with him was over.

It was supper time. Everyone had experienced his or her own personal insights. I explained to Louis about the shifts that I had felt were happening, and how in the light of what was occurring on the earth this was more understandable. Helena began to value her ability to 'channel' – lucky thing – and Sivara was generally excited by the whole business. Louis was characteristically more sensible and grounded, less excitable, but had thoroughly enjoyed our time together.

He gave each of us, in turn, a review of our own lives. I had talked a little to him about my family and shared with him the notion of my 'not going to die', and of course, the ascension process. He was very direct and poignant in his response. Rebecah, he said, was equally bound up with the ascension process, though not overtly, as I was, and this is what bound us in these important times.

There existed, he continued, particularly in England, a class system emanating from the Queen, which was essentially a lie, and kept people unknowingly bound to a limited collective consciousness, both regional and global. Rebecah, despite her limitations of deafness, had overcome huge obstacles and could see in others their unwillingness to overcome theirs. There was a possibility she could become famous, as a TV celebrity, demonstrating to the world that we each have a choice and needn't be limited.

This was interesting, as Rebecah recently gave a talk and slide show on Africa to some students from an underprivileged background. They were riveted to her words, and with the help of Sue, my sister-in-law, and their teacher, were able to see that they too could join Operation Raleigh and do the same. Rebecah had made a huge impression on them, and in fact some have applied to Raleigh International. It had actually never occurred to some of them that they could move away from their council estate! Sue said that they never stopped talking about the demonstration, and the fact that they had seen Rebecah on TV. Sue also received outstanding and apparently unheard of results from them that year. I wonder if Rebecah contributed to the change in attitude which made this possible?

This resonated with Helena, as she too was totally aware of this, particularly in English society. She had heard an inner voice, prior to coming on this trip, from some Native American Indian tribe telling her to leave Canada. She now felt that the purpose was to help redress this imbalance in her work in schools within English society. Sometimes it takes an outsider to see things from a more holistic point of view. Her parentage was English, so she had kept an affinity with the English way of life.

There was, he continued, in Rebecah's presence, something magnanimous and captivating, which went beyond words, but was possibly greater than words in its power to penetrate deep into the heart of what was really important, rather like, as mentioned earlier, the dolphins and whales. Rebecah would, he said, at some stage join forces with me actively in my ascension work.

We ended the day with a brief discussion about Christ. I had asked him if he thought that the whole Christ story was true and if it was, why could we not aspire to such heights – even the best of us – and by that I meant the Tibetan lamas and Indian avatars and other such people. His reply didn't wholly surprise me. He said that a man possessed of such abilities, like the miracle cures, possibly would not be born of woman, or with the genetic DNA we currently possess as a human race. The birth process would, by natural law, involve the forgetting process.

Christ, if indeed he did exist, would have been created by far superior beings, and brought here in an adult form and probably left in the desert, to be occupied by a highly evolved entity with the power to connect with his higher self and thereby remember everything. Such beings could well be amongst us now but would not come to our notice unless it was deemed right for it to be so. The stories of the Virgin Birth, the shepherds, the dates, twelve Apostles and the rest, had been used many times in the history of the planet and were highly symbolic. Like all religions, the stories provided, firstly, underlying truths to give credibility, and secondly, nonsense, to keep people in a state of love light and cluelessness in order to be controllable.

As for the Ascension, perhaps, as the Mayans believed, it was possible to refine the vibrations of the body so that they would seem to disappear, but just be outside our range of vision – rather like the astral or spirit body of a dying person. Such practices, he continued, would involve knowledge of how not to eat, taking in only prana from the air, a conscious rising of the kundalini energy, and a constantly held awareness of a oneness with all things.

All this was just an interesting hypothesis for me, as I had no actual knowledge of the truth of his words. One thing I *did* know was that my soul's growth depended on experience and not belief systems. Sometimes those experiences were pleasant and sometimes distinctly the opposite. For me, soul growth meant moving towards knowing who I was, why I was here and what my life's purpose was. Most of all it meant love, as in lack of fear and less judgement of others. Happily for me, judgement of others was falling away naturally. It was a case of noticing that I would judge but not condemn.

However, when the presence of the eternal is experienced, love energy flows and spontaneous miracles can follow. Anyone could attain this. First, one must have desire for this; second forgiveness and compassion, including self; third, the surrender of thought and desire to God, leading to emptiness of mind to be filled with a blissful oneness. All teachings, he said, stemmed from this experience.

He then made a detour in his dignified delivery, interjecting something quite strange and new to us. 'There exists, and has existed for aeons, an insidious force at the root of all major religions and governments, which feeds off fear and human sacrifice, particularly the sacrifice of children.' This information, he added, was now being exposed on the Internet. Once you know, then your subconscious cannot be bombarded through incessant propaganda and you can be free! Here his expression changed and his demeanour threw forward a gentle yet powerful admonishment. 'Do not assume that all information of value is "pretty". You need to know what is *really* going on!'

I wanted to ask much more but felt instinctively that logistical details were irrelevant and that I could do further research myself. For the moment it was the essence of the message that was important, so I confined myself to one last question.

'What do we do?'

His reply was thus. 'Your inner guidance tells you. For example, you have already come into contact with breatharians, haven't you?' This was true, I had met two of them myself. 'You know, therefore, that something is pointing you in that direction, yes? You now know that the major players in governments are lying, do you not? Do not be complacent!'

Just as suddenly as that severe, one-pointed thrust had emerged, it vanished, to be replaced by the more 'loving' approach, to which we had grown accustomed.

'But, you know, the whole consciousness of the planet is rising, and soon – probably within your lifetimes – you will see miracles, you will shift dimensions, you will have knowledge, or gnosis about the mysteries of life! Whilst it is true that time as such does not exist and that all your past and future lives exist simultaneously in this "now" time, there is, paradoxically, a time for everything. Just as you would not try to speed up the gestation of a baby in the womb, or expect a May blossom to appear in October, so your lives and all living things are bound up with the planets and their orbits, which have their timings and their influence upon you is profound; until it is not. The web of life here on earth is all encompassing; until it is not.'

That said, he then played a tape for us of something quite exquisite. It sounded like heavenly choirs, singing in harmony with non-human voices. We all listened, enraptured, and it was a fitting way to end the session. I since learned that this was a tape of crickets changed, en masse, to a different frequency. The wonder of the universe was captured!

This felt like the closest to the truth I had come, and it felt immensely satisfying. Another part of my journey was over, and it was home to England with Rebecah and the rest of my family.

Rebecah, Part Two

RETURNING, ONCE AGAIN, TO REBECAH'S STORY, AS SOON AS she had completed her university course, she made her trip to Africa, where she went on to experience many poignant incidents. By far the scariest was her encounter with a wild boar. She was staying at the school for the deaf with Katrina, a friend from England who was, like Rebecah, deaf, and who had raised money to help the school. Together they had ventured out on a bike ride and taken a forbidden detour. They came almost face to face with a wild boar. Fear gripped them but Rebecah took charge, indicating to Katrina to keep absolutely still. I think that they probably both prayed, but off in the distance appeared a herd of zebra. The boar was distracted and turned in search of more interesting prey. Rebecah, as she described it, looked up to the sky and said, 'Thank you, God.' No more detours!

Prior to this incident she had gone on a walk, again with Katrina, to find a water spring, which was situated in a somewhat unusual and beatific setting. The track was a little difficult to follow and they found themselves facing a very steep incline. Rebecah told Katrina to remain put while she investigated. Somehow a young African man got their attention and in universal sign language, with strong gestures, told her to go no further. The three of them came together for a chat and he recounted his tale.

Just in that spot where they were heading were cheetahs and lions. He had been caught by one. At that point he lifted his kaftan to reveal a huge scar. The beast had tossed him in the air and he had fallen harshly, only to hit his head on a rock. He landed on his ear. The result – deafness! Rebecah has a photograph of this man.

Rebecah, at this point in my story, has now reached the grand age of twenty-five. She has a job and as she gains confidence and responsibility is enjoying life more and more. I talked to her a little about the ascension of the planet as I often do, about two weeks ago. I told her that my friend Joyce, who is incredibly psychic, had said that she would be involved with me in doing some important ascension planetary work. Her reply was simply, 'I know I will.' When I wrote the section at the beginning of 'my story' on how Rebecah's and my lives were to come together in connection with my own personal purpose, I didn't know what I was going to say, but everything unfolded as it naturally does. So in what I consider to be my last round on earth, it's significant that Rebecah and I have chosen to play the roles of mother and daughter, and that we will both be involved at some level with ascension. Why, I ask myself, has she chosen to be deaf?

I think the answer to this question – and let me state clearly, that I don't 'know' the answer, but can only speculate – is a mixture of things. About six months ago, I interpreted a psychic reading for Rebecah, and Claire, the person doing the reading, said that Rebecah had used words destructively in a past life and had decided to make sure that she didn't do it again. If this was true then Rebecah's deafness is karmic, which I find most credible. Many of the physical ailments which we carry with us are karmic, I believe. Certainly they are that, or genetic. However, these things are only beliefs, they are not true knowledge, and whilst it can at times be frustrating not to know the reasons for things, it can allow for greater compassion, which is a cherished quality in earth beings, and one which encompasses all that we need to have in order to grow.

Talking of compassion, I promised to share with you a little of my experience with the older generation of deaf people. It is most interesting to see how we, as a nation – and of course, other nations, too – have grown greatly in our compassion towards the deaf, and I will try to illustrate this point. My first encounter with a deaf person was with the next-door neighbours of a boyfriend I had at the tender age of seventeen. It was the wife who was deaf and the husband was hearing. My reaction was one of preferred avoidance, but when that became impossible, I found myself having to make a direct and active attempt at communication, or else be unspeakably rude and uncaring. I felt embarrassed and inadequate, and on reflection realised that my boyfriend had the capacity to be much more real and upfront than I did. That was a lesson in itself, as I'm sure I was a truer representative of the majority of the population.

I remember her telling me that the bow in my ponytail was too heavy, which was why it was slipping out. She offered me some chiffon, a much lighter fabric, which I didn't like at all. I didn't think that she would understand if I gave her my point of view and saw her kindness, and I think – nay, I hope – I graciously accepted. Nowadays, I would have the courage to say what I thought, kindly, and in sign language, so that there would be total understanding and no condescension on either part.

My next little story is a very significant one. It must be in the order of twenty years ago that I had joined a group of people known simply as 'friends of the deaf'. They comprised a group of hearing people, social workers and deaf people, some of whom were from Durham University. This in itself should have told me something; you don't make it to Durham University on a song and a prayer. One young man in particular stood out. He couldn't speak yet but was doing a PhD in physics. We went for a rowing-boat trip on the river, and he could see that I was a little hesitant, to say the least. He totally took charge, reassured me, held me, calmed me down and took the oars from me as I continued to quiver. (Water and me never have been the best of friends.)

When the trip ended we went on to the university campus for a social gathering, including charades. The rest of us may as well have not played. This same young man was so sharp it became a one-man band and he had to back down. It was truly an insight for me and my whole perspective on the deaf changed from that time. They were not to be helped but cooperated with on an equal footing. Yes, they may need practical help, like with the use of a telephone, or explanation of the written word; but it wasn't the sort of 'holier than thou' type of help that I had unconsciously felt I needed to give. 'Help without condescension' would be a better way of putting it. This may seem obvious to many of the readers, but to me it was a revelation.

A lady who is a teacher of the deaf and who is herself deaf told her story to us with the aid of an interpreter. It was part of our introduction to 'deaf culture' in our stage one sign language classes. Nora grew up in the North East and left school with very little in the way of speech. On leaving school she was directed to many jobs, most of them fairly practical in nature and none of which reflected what she really wanted to do. One such job was in a factory as a seamstress. She had asked for guidance for a particular task, as she felt that the instructions were wrong, but try as she might nobody was willing to help her. When she *did* carry out the instructions, they were indeed wrong. One of the other workers told her that she would go to prison and Nora believed her. She was mortified.

This story is indicative of the isolation and lack of understanding of life through limited language that many deaf people no doubt experience. However, Nora took qualifications later in life to become a very successful teacher of sign language, and she was certainly on the ball when teaching me. Very little escaped her notice. However, when she was asked if things had improved, she said that she thought they hadn't really. I have to say that I disagree with her, and her own career is an indication of this. We may still have a long way to go – especially in fulfilling the demands of the deaf that all people learn sign language – but we've come a long way too.

There is something which the deaf can use to their advantage called 'Access to Work', which includes the provision of interpreters and people to help them with language skills so that they are not stifled in their choice of work. I think Nora would have benefited greatly from this, had it then been available, but it is available now, so let us not say that progress has not been made, and rejoice in it, so to speak.

A book recently came to my notice entitled *The Raging Quiet*. It is a fictional book, set in mediaeval times, written by Sherryl Jorah.

The book can be summated as follows: Marnie is a newcomer to the village and her husband dies suddenly. She is treated with suspicion. Raver too is an outcast, and dubbed the village lunatic. The two become friends and they develop a sign language, as Raver is not mad, but deaf. Raver becomes calmer, but rather than see this as a victory, the villagers try Marnie for witchcraft.

Here is a quote from the book:

> 'That's your name,' he said, showing it to her.
>
> For a long time Marnie studied her name. Then, very carefully, she made the sign she had decided on: the first letter of her name, traced with her forefinger over her heart. Then she said to Raven, 'Marnie is my name. What people call me.'
>
> 'You are a woman,' Raven said.
>
> 'There are many women. Every one has a different name. My name is Marnie.'
>
> As always, she spoke as she signed, and Father Brannan observed Raven's reaction. He saw how Marnie watched Raven's lips, as well as the graceful movements of her hands, and how the youth's face was solemn and attentive, comprehending everything. The priest shook his head, marvelling, hardly able to believe that this was the mad Raver of Torcurra, for years flogged for his devils and mindless savagery.

Here is the author's own comment on the book:

> All my life I have felt a great affinity with deaf people, and have loved sign language. For several years I worked with profoundly deaf children in schools, and spoke with them through signs. Marnie's dealings with Raven – her difficulties, frustration, despair, joy and triumph – are all things I have experienced.

The author's affinity with the deaf, and her deep understanding of those children she taught, suggest to me that in part she was tapping into a past life when she wrote this book, and it may not have been quite so fictional as one might think.

A similar situation is encapsulated in a play, written by the author of *Children of Silence*, Kathy Robinson. One scene depicts a Dickensian-type school, and a doctor arrives with a brutal determination to make those children hear! He attempts to apply his 'new-found' skill and ends up puncturing the eardrum of a deaf child. This is done with such savagery that death occurs. I cried whilst watching that scene. There was something so plausible about it. The play was performed in a theatre in Stockton with an almost exclusively deaf cast. It was very well attended, too, which was heartening.

Finally, before moving from the subject of children with a difference, I'd like to say a little about indigo children. These children have been named such because those with the ability to see auras can see that this is what they have in common with each other; i.e. that they have an indigo coloured aura. Those readers who are interested can find much information on the Internet or from a book entitled *The Indigo Children* by Lee Carroll and Jan Tober, and *The Care and Feeding of Indigo Children* by Doreen Virtue. To categorise them in ways other than by their aura is rather difficult, as their behaviour is so varied, but here is an attempt.

They feel a right to be here and equality with adults. Being told what to do is not an option. They prefer creativity to orthodox or institutionalised behaviour. They are often psychic and outspoken and sometimes outrageous in their behaviour.

I believe that they are here to make people think about what we are forcing our children to do, particularly in schools. This is a complex subject and it is not in the nature of this book to detail all the facts. It would be impossible anyway. They are children who display unusual psychological attributes. They are often diagnosed as ADD or ADHD, though not all indigo children with this diagnosis are indigo. Drugs are used to suppress them and when you see their behaviour it is not difficult to see why, yet drugs are so damaging and can suppress their lovely side too. Drugs like Ritalin can also lead to more serious addictions in later life.

It seems to me that the extremes of duality, of the good and the bad, are here starkly coexisting. These children need sensitive handling and skilled parenting.

They will benefit from special help like, for instance, homeopathy, rather than drugs, and a skilled therapist who is highly aware. They do not respond to the rules and discipline required in normal schooling and will rebel when these are inflicted upon them. Children are being forced to use their heads all the time. In schools today it is *force, force, force* – and they've had enough! We need love with our technology, love with our creative skills, and we need to stop inculcating the idea of failure if we don't think in a prescribed way. It could well be that there are deaf indigo children – another double whammy! I would, however, like to add that many children in schools are difficult to teach they are so naughty, and teachers deserve medals.

It is now time for Rebecah to add something of her own story and here it is:

How Rebecah Sees Life

My University Years

1ST YEAR

During my first year in university, I struggled big time because I altered my course from art to science. I had to go back as far as GCSE level for background understanding as a science degree was a big jump for me. I stayed up very late each night until 1 or 2 a.m. as I wished to be satisfied that I had understood all the necessary steps. English was (still is) a challenging confrontation. However, I did enjoy some of my social life and made new friends with hearing people.

2ND YEAR

I was still hard at work and continued to struggle, but my strength sustained. I moved to an inner campus where there were more deaf people. Here I felt much more at ease, as there was a deaf community.

3RD YEAR

My best friend Colette and I shared a flat for one whole year and I loved every moment of our time spent together. I felt very free. However, she went away nearly every weekend to be with her boyfriend and that saddened me.

The study itself was becoming more interesting but mentally I had 'had it'. It was far too much work for me, in fact it was overload. I wanted to give up so badly, and couldn't cope with the workload.

My English grammar had to be improved as I'd not kept up with it. The standard expected of me as a third year student was too much. Sometimes I cried and really wanted to quit but my instincts told me not to because I was so very determined to achieve my degree. And I did.

Once my university ended, off I dashed to Africa for six and a half months travelling. I had been sponsored by the Winston Churchill Trust to do a nine week stint in conservation work in Tanzania. This I hated. It was not the work itself that I hated as I have a great caring for the planet, but once again, I felt so lonely and totally left out within an all-hearing environment. There were twenty-three people doing the work, including staff, but I was the only deaf person.

When laughter came, none told me what was going on. When night-time came the only form of lighting was in the form of old-fashioned lanterns which didn't provide a strong enough light to enable me to read people's lips, therefore I was not able to catch up with what they were saying. So, I trailed off to my bed, picked up a book and read till I got tired. My head tourch was damn useful and I brought an excess of batteries which I knew I would use. I read lots of books to kill the time and counted the remaining days of my volunteer work.

I couldn't wait to 'bogg off' from the camp. The staff were not helpful and not aware of my deafness, with the exception of one. One of the volunteers was brilliant with me and acted as an excellent signer/interpreter, but after seven weeks she got fed up with me. I didn't blame her and totally understood her patience .It is hard work being with a deaf person within a hearing community.

However, travelling with pals I had made, or travelling individually, was, 'beyond excitement'. I felt a freedom that I've not felt in all of my 'studying' life, from aged three and a half, to aged twenty-three; non stop! I could choose where and when to visit the countries of my choice. Nobody was telling me what to do!

Although attending both art college and university were my options, as I had wanted to achieve my highest academic standard, I was now left alone, in the mountains and beyond!

Life Now

My upbringing as a deaf person has been fine. I feel quite content in that area. I always felt very loved so the whole deal was not a problem. As I grew older and became more independent, I realised how important it was for me to be in the deaf community. We don't meet each other every day, like hearing people, so any special occasions, I'd feel I'd have to be there. I can always enjoy the company of deaf people, as I don't have to rely on lips. My signing is fluent and natural and so is theirs.

Work

At work, they provide 'Access To Work' (ATW) which is very efficient. I don't know what I would do without them. They help me big time at work. If I have written a report or letter, they check the grammar before I submit it. Interpreters are provided for communication between deaf and hearing people. Deaf people then do not have to struggle in lip-reading hearing people. Even at vital meetings, interpreters are present so that we know what is going on. Deaf people are able to have their say.

My job at present is a 'BSL translator/interpreter' under Signpost, contracted to Tyne Tees T., transmitting on Digital and ITV. I am a trainee, but hopefully, in the future, I can become involved with environmental issues within Signpost, because nature is my first love.

The story doesn't end here but rather forms the finale to a chapter in Rebecah's life. It is the end of childhood and the beginning of adult existence, which as we all know brings on its own set of challenges and opportunities for growth. Sometimes I feel that we are living on borrowed time. My vision for my children certainly doesn't extend beyond this.

Does Rebecah want children? Does she worry in case they are deaf? She's not worried. Neither am I. My vision does, however, embrace a more peaceful and loving world; one where the lion can lie down with the lamb. Naive? I certainly hope so. It is in being vulnerable that I have extended my boundaries to expect the unexpected, and I hope to create the uncreateable. I have no doubt that Rebecah will help me in this endeavour. The next chapter in our lives is yet to be written, but for now, just for now, it has a very happy ending.

Monarch, warrior and dear soul mate
The work is nearly complete
and you and I will see it through
Yea, until eternity yields Her crown
and rests in the still point of creation.

Time will loosen its shackles
and doors are to open with a roar
and blinding light.

Beating within the womb
The sound of the Constant One's heartbeat
Trembling to rejoin
The Master beckons, Come!
lean on me for you are weary now.
Rest.
The Dawn is near.

Ananiti

Printed in the United Kingdom
by Lightning Source UK Ltd.
103732UKS00001B/166-168

9 781844 012565